FINISH TO THE SKY

THE GOLF SWING MOE NORMAN TAUGHT ME:
GOLF KNOWLEDGE WAS HIS GIFT TO ME.

by

Greg Lavern

Table of Contents

IMPORTANT QUOTES FROM MOE NORMAN

Believe in yourself and don't be afraid to make it happen.

There is nothing in this world you have to do unless you want to do it.

You are what you think you are: a winner or a loser. Winners look up and losers look down.

If you did something before you can do it again; learn from experience.

When you have lack of awareness you have fear to win or play to your ability.

The practice tee to the first tee is the longest walk in golf.

When you learn to visualize, everything gets easier. I could see the results before the ball hit the ground.

The secret to golf or anything in life is hard work. That can never be replaced.

Learn and play with someone better than yourself.

The largest room in the house is the room for improvement.

Flow with nature and just go do it.

Bad thinking, bad shots.

Be aware of your surroundings so you can find your comfort zone.

Don't put pressure on yourself when hitting a shot; it's only a damn golf ball.

Always hit through the golf ball not to it.

When I set-up to the golf ball I start by building my house with a solid foundation.

Vanity is the luxury of fools.

I swing within the golf course never out of bounds.

Love your driver, wedge and putter as your best friends.

Everyone hits bad shots and the one that hits fewer usually wins.

ACKNOWLEDGEMENTS

To Lawson Mitchell for his introduction to Moe Norman in 1974 and his contribution of the 1963-64 videos of Moe for my book Finish To The Sky. His distinguished club professional career and relationship with tour players has developed him into one of the most knowledgeable teachers in the United States. I thank him for his close friendship all these years.

To Tim Lynch who had the desire and deep dedication to learn Moe's true golf swing and has been a student of mine since the time he flew me out to teach him in 2009. Tim's ambition was to get the true golf swing that Moe taught me out to the golfing public without personal gain. I can't thank him enough for his great work to improve the quality of the video and still photos. I highly recommend him for his photo reconditioning. Tim has been an honest friend who totally supported my efforts to get this book out. His efforts and friendship are greatly appreciated.

Ian MacMillan is a man of truth and integrity who provided continual friendship especially when I really needed him. Through the direction of God, Ian and his awesome wife demonstrated their goodness and strong dedication as true Christians. I was blown away and totally impressed with their kindness. Praise God! Ian is an excellent software developer that produced the early video projects of myself and comparison videos of Moe and did the editing and proof reading for the final manuscript.

Daniel Dupuis for his great still photos of my golf swing. Daniel is an excellent photographer and his work can be viewed at info@pinkfrogphotography.com.

To Diwata Buenaventura Tordil for being an honest true friend full of encouragement.

Thank you to the supporters and followers of Moe Norman that recognize and appreciate his great talent for striking the golf ball and willingness to learn.

Moe Norman for being my best friend and golf mentor who was the best of the best. His memory and teachings will stay with me forever.

FOREWORD

Moe Norman knew his golf swing and could explain it like Einstein knew the theory of relativity!

When it came to hitting a golf ball pure Moe kept his knowledge close to him. However, he did share his unique approach of the golf swing with two trusted friends. It all started in the sixties with Lawson Mitchell and during the seventies and eighties I became involved with the private execution of the golf swing with Moe Norman. I certainly appreciated Lawson's recommendation that led to my introduction to the straightest striker of the golf ball in the world during 1974.

Moe was a character and "smart as a fox" who never told anything of importance to anyone else despite the different people that claimed friendship with Moe or wanted a piece of him. These promoters of Moe Norman's pure action thought he neither understood his golf swing nor could explain it. Nothing could be further from the truth.

These foolish advocates that promoted Moe did not understand his golf swing and were the same individuals that he never shared his important mechanics or actual knowledge with.

The lengthy conversations, playing and practicing with our close friend Moe Norman, gave us great insight and understanding to Moe's character. From the golf knowledge passed on to us, especially the way he explained his golf swing, clearly demonstrated that Moe was not autistic. It is quite possible he had a social disorder from being lonely and rejected throughout his early years or a frightening experience from an unfortunate accident in childhood.

When Moe was with his inner circle he felt comfortable with an integrity that could set an example for many people. From my ongoing relationship of practice and playing golf with Moe Norman, I learned that Moe had great respect for the talent of Ben Hogan and Byron Nelson. I once asked Moe who was a better ball striker, Hogan or you? Moe said, "I am, Hogan was great in his own way." Moe wished he had the opportunity to see Byron when he won 11 professional golf tournaments in a row. Moe had great respect for Byron Nelson even as a youngster and complimented him with his unique golf swing.

Rather than splitting hairs, I can certainly attest that Moe Norman had some Hogan and Nelson in the golf swing he taught to Lawson and myself that we decided to pass on to the golf community. Ben Hogan, a favorite of many, once said, "If you hit it straight it is an accident." Moe replied, "Ben, you will be seeing lots of accidents today." Hogan in an interview said, "Moe Norman is the only golfer I would walk across the street to watch." It is beyond a shadow of a doubt that both men had great respect for each other's talent for striking the golf ball.

Greatness was achieved through dedication, hard work and respect for a game that both men dedicated the majority of their life to.

Great ball strikers like Lee Trevino and VJ Singh have expressed their opinions for years of how pure and straight Moe Norman hits the golf ball. When fine ball strikers from both the regular tour and senior tour give Moe the highest praise for his talent and ability it is time to listen and learn from this book. I personally would like to thank Lee Trevino and VJ Singh for their dedication to our close friend and teacher. Moe gave the highest of praise to both of these talented players and enjoyed their company any time he was around them.

This book will help many golfers, both professional and amateur alike, to become better ball strikers with the knowledge passed on to us from the straightest golfer that ever put his hands on a golf club. There are many things the conventional golfer can take from Moe Norman's approach to the golf swing that will truly allow you to play great golf. Moe concentrated on purity of technique and could hit it long at will from hitting the golf ball so solid. I highly recommend the Moe Norman golf swing as Moe performed it in the 1960's and 70's. This is the way he taught me.

All golfers should seriously study closely if your desire is to hit the ball straight and pure.

Moe approached the golf swing his own way where he did many things during the downswing that complimented the action of many great ball strikers throughout history.

Greg Lavern

INTRODUCTION OF THE WORLD'S STRAIGHTEST BALL STRIKER MOE NORMAN

I grew up learning that the only time your golf score really matters is during competition and heard the popular golf line many times that it's not how, but how many. To me the object of the game was to hit the fairway and green through dedicated practice in an attempt to hit the golf ball at an intended target. Target golf was my entire focus during my many rewarding practice sessions. I concentrated on Moe Norman's exclusive teaching or ball striking demonstrations. It was great fun while the sweat became inspirational to enhance my daily practice for many hours hitting a variety of numerous shots. Striving for a consistent pattern of shot making developed my thought process each day that motivated me for the following morning for more improvement.

The Master ball-striker Moe Norman provided life lessons that developed an open mind and built a good attitude to accept the good with the bad. It made sense to me that the best approach was to hit the golf ball straight so it would become much easier to score. At times I could hit the golf ball straight with soft landing and demonstrated characteristics toward purity of technique. The challenge was to bring my good shots from the practice tee to the golf course known by many as the longest walk in golf. Moe made me aware early in our relationship that distance is created through maximum speed at impact while accuracy requires the proper sequence of motion, of hitting your positions to maintain good balance throughout the entire swing. Moe's unique style suited my make-up and toned my moves. The idea of a pretty swing was thrown out the door. Moe would say, "The golf swing means nothing, hit your positions." Hitting your positions to get the club head on the ball was his main concentration for consistency. When the proper positions were achieved the accuracy and grace, particularly in Moe's golf swing, became a beautiful flowing action to watch. If you were a student of the game, then you would become witness to poetry in motion.

When Moe walked up the middle of the fairway he would sing in a high voice "Poetry in motion, how I love it so, poetry in motion, is what I do so well." Moe had the flow. His tempo and timing was smooth and would stride to the beat of his own drummer. Moe would say, "I walk with both toes pointing down the fairway straight, not outward like horny duck." To know Moe was to love him as a person who always had a humorous comment or expression to describe a situation. Moe was a colorful character that walked the middle of the fairway in plain, polka dot or striped attire despite the opinion of others that may have found fault some days with his non-matching wardrobe.

Moe was a unique individual that valued his freedom to play golf without the involvement of dating a girlfriend to spend time with. Moe figured it would not be fair to him or her and avoided this kind of lifestyle. When his golf day came to an end he accepted his loneliness and did other things to occupy his time. Moe was dedicated to hard work with his focus on what he was trying to achieve. Striking the golf ball and kissing his golf clubs rather than the girls became his desire.

Moe would say, "I tried my best and became a pretty good player and maybe the best ball striker in the world." Moe displayed a huge black callus on his left hand with a tear in his eye when telling me that he gave it his best and never gave up. Then Moe said with a smile, "The best pair of hands that ever held a golf stick, I have what millions of people want, I know how to hit the golf ball pure every day when I get out of bed."

It is a tragedy that people did not make the effort to understand him even though Moe made a mockery of the game through sheer talent. Times have now changed, and many people around the world are showing a great interest in Moe Norman. The majority of golfers want to become better ball strikers and learn the actual way Moe Norman swung the club in his prime when he was really ripe.

Greg Lavern

Chapter 1 –
The Early Years: My Teacher and Friend Moe!

It all started at the end of the 1973 golf season when I was a young golf professional from the Weston G.C. in Toronto, Canada. My tremendous love for the game and desire to become the best ball striker I could, encouraged winter practice in Florida, USA. With a letter of introduction from head professional Gordon Delatt, my adventurous heart directed me to Tomoka Oaks G.C. in Ormond Beach, Florida. I decided to fly down since it was my first year south and I was unfamiliar with my destination. On arrival I took a cab, with my golf clubs, suitcase, and cheerful smile, immediately to the golf course. Once I walked through the golf shop door I was greeted by a gentleman who was nicely dressed in golf attire and welcomed me. The gentleman introduced himself as head professional, Lawson Mitchell, who mentioned he once lived in Toronto, Canada before he became a resident of Florida. He easily recognized my Canadian accent. I showed Lawson my letter of introduction that stated my name with a brief explanation that I would be starting in the golf business on my return back to Canada. I asked Lawson how much is the monthly fee? Lawson replied, "Just practice and work hard and we will worry about any fees later." I thanked Lawson and told him I would practice hard and hoped he could take a look at my swing after a few practice sessions.

It soon would be dusk so Lawson made a phone call to a lady that just happened to have an available room for my winter stay. This was the same rooming house Moe Norman stayed in for years when playing Tomoka Oaks called Ryles Inn.

I told Lawson I never met Moe Norman on a personal basis though I caddied for a golf professional from Quebec who was paired with Moe in the second round. I asked Lawson what type of man was Moe? Lawson laughed and said, "Different."

It was time to head to the rooming house, so Lawson drove me to meet the land lady, Mrs. Ryles, who welcomed me with open arms. Lawson had to get back to the club and told me to meet him on the practice tee tomorrow morning. I thanked my new friend Lawson and appreciated his help in getting me settled.

Once Lawson left, Mrs. Ryles showed me a room nicely decorated with a southern flare. There was a Holy Bible placed on my bed that told me I was in a religious home and this nice lady deserved respect and good manners in return during my stay. It was a long day of travel so I thanked the hostess and headed to bed.

Early next morning I went straight to the back shop and filled a huge yellow range pail with three or four hundred balls. It was so great; I was allowed to hit all the balls I wanted. You could say I was in my glory since hard work never bothered me and I could hit golf balls for hours. It was satisfaction to gaze down the practice fairway covered with dew at the hundreds of white practice balls glowing after sunrise. Some mornings I would be the only golfer hitting balls with total concentration on what I was trying to achieve.

My practice session was going smoothly when Lawson Mitchell showed up in his golf cart to see how I was making out. This showed the professionalism of the man who not only gave me the opportunity to practice and play but took an interest in my progress. Lawson just sat in the golf cart and watched as I proceeded to hit different clubs and a variety of shots. I was informed my natural ability was second to none though there were a few things I could work on to make my ball striking better. I asked Lawson if there was anything I should work on now that he had seen me hit the ball Lawson said, "I will let you know, I got to go." I was excited from the attention Lawson gave me and that encouraged my morning practice sessions. I prepared a normal routine of morning practice and playing nine holes in the afternoon to combine play and practice.

It was easy to locate me near the practice tee from 7:00 am till noon every morning, and Lawson always knew where to find me to pass on his incredible understanding of the golf swing. Lawson was one of the finest teachers in Florida. He was respected by Canadian tour stars Ken Venning, Herb Holzsheiter, and of course, Moe Norman, who highly respected his talent as a teaching professional and player. Even young hopefuls attempting to play well on the mini tours did not hesitate to seek help on swing mechanics from Lawson.

Lawson was an excellent striker of the golf ball that shined from his ability to hit a baseball during his professional career. Playing for the old Toronto Maple Leaf organization, he was selected by the Chicago White Sox though his knees gave out. Still with the ability to hit a baseball, he helped young prospects breaking into the professional ranks to improve their hitting performance. When hitting a golf ball, he hit it solid and was considered a long hitter particularly with the driver. His golf swing displayed balance and tempo while his bottom half would start the downswing with passive hands that allowed him to fade or draw the golf ball at will. His teachings included top notch sound fundamentals.

From the many practice sessions I experienced with Lawson Mitchell, he insisted on striking the golf ball solid and pure under pressure. That made an incredible difference between the average ball striker or a great ball striker. The vast improvement of my own swing included the explanation of how to pick out the little things that most teaching professionals don't easily identify. This also built student confidence with your teacher when he could identify things others couldn't. Much of my own ability to identify the unnoticeable when teaching a golf lesson came from the time I spent with Lawson and expanded with Moe.

It was a beautiful day at the golf course in 1974 during my normal morning practice routine. While hitting balls I noticed a man sitting on the bench close to the putting green reading a book. Once I finished practice on the range I headed over toward the putting green to work on my short game where I noticed he was still reading and watching me being as conspicuous as possible. Suddenly the man on the bench came up to me with a soft voice and asked if I would like to play a few holes around 4:00pm.

I introduced myself to my new playing partner who introduced himself as Moe Norman. I said to Mr. Norman as we walked toward the first tee that I heard how great he hit the golf ball. Moe responded, "Watch." Before I could say anything he had four balls launched down the middle of the fairway with the same trajectory while I stood, flabbergasted. This was a tough act to follow though I wanted to bring my practice to the first tee and hit my first two balls down the middle then started to walk down the fairway when Moe told me to hit a couple more. "I hit four, so should you." As we proceeded down the fairway I asked Moe why he wanted to play golf with me. Moe said, "I liked what I saw." After our short iron shots to the green we repaired our ball marks before hitting a few putts from different angles on the putting surface.

On the first par-three-hole Moe decided to put on a ball striking clinic into a stiff breeze. Moe went to the back tee and selected a four iron where his first shot hit the flag stick followed by his next two under six feet. Just before he was to hit his last shot I said aloud in fun that I would bet him a Coke he couldn't hole his last one. Well, I learned really fast that you never underestimate Moe Norman.

As he was picking up his tee, Moe casually said, "You owe me a Coke." With much amazement I said, "That was the greatest ball striking exhibition I have ever witnessed; the Cokes are on me."

Walking up the fairway, I asked Moe if he could teach me how to ace. It could come in handy. Moe laughed and started to chase me in good fun. "Come here smart guy, let me teach you, let me teach you."

Moe then replied, "Just lucky it rolled straight like I hit it from the tee." While on the green I rolled in a couple of my tee shots into the hole. Moe said, "Look at your putter blade going to the hole and so steady like the Rock of Gibraltar. Teach me that." "Sure, anything I can help you with Moe." I told Moe to allow the right shoulder to go under his chin on his follow through and hold his putter face at the hole on his finish.

Moe started to make it from everywhere and continued to practice this putting tip for the rest of the round with total concentration.

| GREG LAVERN

It was magical to watch someone hit the golf ball that solid with every drive down the middle, while iron shots would cover the flag, just the way a golf ball should be struck with beautiful flight.

Moe would take bacon strips with his irons and never hamburger divots the way other professional golfers executed their shots.

I learned a tremendous amount every time Moe moved into the golf ball with authority and grace that you could watch all day long. Moe told me, when you play four balls a hole you will experience different shots and build a repetitive swing. "Score only matters in tournaments when you have to play one ball; then it counts."

Our nine holes ended with a handshake as we headed to the clubhouse for the Coke I owed Moe for his incredible ace. We talked golf for a few hours after our round until the clubhouse and pro shop were about to close.

It was getting late and Moe knew I was from Toronto, Canada and invited me to eat with him at Morrisons, the buffet style eating place. Moe wanted to eat there for the spaghetti, meatballs, liver and onions, or roast beef, all you could eat for three bucks. Both of us resided in Toronto, Canada, during the summer months and took the opportunity to know each other much better with some general conversation after dinner.

Moe suggested we go for a drive in his car just to talk with no special destination planned. I had many questions for Moe and he had plenty for me. I was given my first tour of the area since Moe knew where most places were from his coming down for years. We visited golf courses, shopping malls, and good and bad parts of town while we talked golf and got to know each other much better.

Moe told me he stayed at Ryles Inn for years which was a great deal for $80.00 a month if down for a long time playing golf with only meals to buy. By the way, Moe paid for dinner at Morrison's and told me that I was buying next time. The many times we would eat together Moe happily grabbed the bill since he knew I needed my money to stay for our winter golf together. I would surprise him sometimes and unexpectedly pick up the tab, something that Moe appreciated very much.

We were good to each other while working hard on our golf.

While driving around Moe told me that he was learning about the golf mind from teachers likes Irv Sloch, Bob Toski and Paul Bertholy. I was given written material while we listened to tapes of these teachers on the mind.

I often wondered who could teach this great striker of the golf ball when he drives it perfect and hits the majority of iron shots ten feet from the hole. Moe would say, "The golf swing is 20%, and the mind is 80%" while pointing to his head. I asked Moe why he was studying, Moe responded, "Greg, never stop learning. I will become a golf analyst when I finish my studies. I wish I knew in the beginning what I know now, I would have won more tournaments. It's like I have been born again." I absorbed Moe's new insight with great interest and would ask questions on the comments these teachers were making. To have the opportunity to be around this master ball striker, who knows his own swing and can demonstrate easily, motivated my attention to everything Moe revealed to me.

It was getting late, and Moe drove me back to Ryles Inn where I was staying. I thanked Moe for the fun time we had hanging out together. Moe said, "Thanks pal, I had a nice time, see you tomorrow on the putting green around 10:00 a.m."

Moe showed up the next morning with a jolly smile on his face and wanted to putt a few before we got into striking the ball. He wanted me to hit a few putts for him to study how my shoulder worked under my chin during the putting stroke. Moe quickly praised what he was watching, "Oh, so great, such a natural motion, just like the rock of Gibraltar with the blade so square while the left hand never breaks down." Moe then proceeded to stroke a bunch of putts attempting to imitate my stroke, immediately getting the ball to turn over. Moe was so excited how the ball was coming off the putter face and wanted to know how I took the putter back. I explained to my buddy Moe that the top of the shoulders take the putter back, keeping the hands passive while the right shoulder goes under the chin that causes the putter face to extend in the hole. Moe said, "I am finally getting a pure feeling on the green." You could see the joy and excitement in Moe's eyes who graciously thanked me many times. Moe said, "Greg, you don't know how great this is, so simple and pure. Just think of the tournaments I would have won putting like this if I knew what I know now."

Once we exhausted the putting green, Moe said, "Now it's my turn to give you a lesson, let's go to the speedway where I practice." The speedway is at the Daytona 500 grass parking area that is wide open to hit the golf ball until race season starts around March break. Moe quickly dumped his big bowling bag filled with Titleist golf balls. Before I could say anything he launched a golf ball like an arrow and within a few seconds his second ball was on its way. I watched for the first fifteen minutes the purest drives you could imagine hit right on the nose on target. Moe said, "What am I doing wrong?"

"Nothing! Moe do you ever get tired of hitting it great anytime you practice or play?"

Moe stopped and took a sip of his Coke telling me, "Greg, straight is the way I learned and what I want, though you can always improve in some way. Each day becomes a new challenge."

Moe divided his golf balls so I could practice beside him, shot for shot and swing for swing, in an attempt to hit each shot in the smallest pile possible. He wanted me to visualize the shot before I hit it at my target. Good tempo and balance were at the top of his list, always swinging within himself and that insured good balance. Moe worked on my ball position. He positioned inside my left heel of my wide driver stance and more toward the center with the narrower iron stance. It was important to stay with the shot through impact so your left eye did not move forward pass the ball. Moe would tell me to stay in the batter's box. I was familiar with this description of staying centered that Lawson Mitchell and Moe used in the sixties when experimenting with a golf club and baseball bat. During our practice session Moe took time to show me the positions in the swing he wanted me to hit and work on.

When it was time to pick up our golf shots, we would pull out a wedge and knock any stray balls back into our larger pile with the left arm only. This was good practice to build up left side dominance and left side control. Sometimes Moe would bounce a ball on his wedge while walking to the next ball, long before Tiger Woods displayed his ability of good eye-hand coordination. It was a known fact that Moe could bounce the ball a hundred times without missing a bounce.

The next morning Moe was on the putting green hitting some putts when I asked him if we were going to the speedway today. Moe replied, "Sure, it's a nice day." Once we got to the speedway there was a nice grassy area perfect for practicing our iron shots. Moe started with a seven iron while I watched a few swings where he moved like poetry in motion. Moe could work the ball both ways with a five yard fade or draw with the majority of shots dead straight at his intended target. The amazing thing was his divot, past the ball on the same level with bacon strips, dead square or slightly left. Moe's ball flight would drop straight from the sky like a butterfly, after it ran out of backspin from driver to wedge with a soft landing.

I asked Moe which groove on the club face he would strike the golf ball. Without hesitation while pointing with his finger, "Fourth groove from the bottom as I look under the ball to catch the back of it." Every shot was hit in the middle of the club face. Moe had previously worn out a set of irons during the sixties displayed with black circles the size of a quarter from center face hits.

During my own practice sessions I would work on the same leg action Moe utilized in his swing and that seemed to be my concentration when I hit the golf ball my best. I would push off my right foot and my left knee would lead with the pulling sensation underneath the leg to the target while my right ankle would go down and even roll on the ground. At the speedway Moe liked my leg action and said, "Getting like me." Moe wanted me to start stretching back on the back swing to get the club deeper with more width in position for the club to drop vertically while the legs lead and drive down the line without effort. I stood fairly wide to develop my stance wider like Moe for a solid foundation and proper use of the legs on the downswing. Moe would say, "The left knee sets the arms, hands and shoulders to follow in sequence." Moe knew the golf ball would go where his hands go since he was connected so well.

From our practice session at the speedway I learned there were many aspects of Moe's golf swing I could incorporate to improve my own swing. As I watched Moe hit some four irons into the wind he would bump the ball back towards the center of his stance for a much lower trajectory. Moe would watch his golf ball land softly and would say aloud, "Flight tells all, my left side goes up and right side goes down while my head reverses forming a bow in my right side. Such a simple game." As we walked together to gather up the balls Moe said, "Greg, golf is a game of misses and the fewer misses comes from hitting your positions with repetition."

During our drive home from the speedway Moe started talking about the mind and how it relates to golf. Moe was pleased with how we both struck the golf ball during our practice sessions but now it was time to educate me between the ears. Moe started to speak his mind, "Learn to believe in yourself since most people live on hope and fear, hoping they do well instead of knowing. You have to know yourself and your makeup. Like me, I had color and stood out in tournaments. People would say, 'what will Moe shoot today?', 'How close will he hit it?' or 'what the hell is he going to do next?' Learn to control your emotions so you don't get too high or low, not allowing negative things to enter your mind in tournaments. You have to play with heart and have a gut feeling that winners have," as Moe poked me in the stomach to show me where his feeling was. "I could win when I wanted, when my surroundings were good. Old buddy, you have to want to win and believe in yourself."

I asked Moe if he hit a shot off line how would he get his focus back on track Moe replied, "Forget about it. It's gone. Hit a better one on your next shot; you can only hit one shot at a time. It's a game of misses, miss it quick so the bad shot doesn't clog your mind when you hit your next shot." "How is the studying going Moe?" "I see things from a different perspective with golf and life in general where my comfort zone just isn't on the golf course anymore."

After our talk Moe dropped me off at Ryles Inn, and I thanked him for letting me pick his brain. Moe laughed, "Giving you all my knowledge is my pleasure; just hit it great for me. We have all winter to practice and play, just keep working hard on your game in a smart way. Good thinking, good golf, bad thinking bad golf." Moe gave me some great wisdom that needed to be absorbed and put into action through normal practice and playing, to build confidence in myself and what I was trying to achieve.

The following week I would practice in the morning and play in the afternoon with a pick-up game with some of the members that knew me. Moe was off to see Irv Sloch, a popular teacher of the mind and needed to stop at the club repair shop He always took his clubs in when he needed some equipment repairs or improvements.

It was important for Moe to have his clubs in the best condition possible for his best performance. Before Moe left, he informed me that he would be gone for about a week and we would play late afternoon on his return.

Moe showed up at 4:00 p.m. since his Rolex watch kept perfect time and he was seldom late for any appointment or obligation, particularly a golf commitment. With a jolly smile, Moe said, "Hi pal, the tee is empty and no one ahead of us for three holes." Moe proceeded to strike three balls dead center and you could have laid a blanket over them, without even a practice swing. "Only three balls, did you age on me while you were away?" Moe laughed and said, "I'll show you old, smart guy. It's your turn, now get up there." I hit my four drives down the middle and said, "Hope you don't mind, but I was feeling good and hit an extra one."

Moe said, "Hit all you want, that's how you get better."

"Wish I could hit it straight as an arrow like you."

Moe grabbed me by the arm and said, "I am the best ball striker in the world old buddy. You are on the right track; it takes time and lots of balls. Hogan and myself have it trapped and that takes dedication man, five hundred a day to get to our level. You got it, just work hard so you can repeat every time. A pretty swing means nothing, just hit those positions. Doing great Greg, just keep doing what you are doing and don't change, just refine it. You're getting like me more every day we play." This was encouraging news, especially from Moe Norman who, without a doubt, knew how to put the golf club on the golf ball square every time with confidence. It was so gratifying to me that Moe was passing on his actual moves and thoughts he developed over the years. This was for two reasons, my dedication and my ability to adapt to Moe's movements through trial and error that eventually became natural to me.

Moe sometimes would leave me in limbo to figure things out for myself since he wanted me to think but would always tell me right from wrong if I asked. When I figured things out to his satisfaction; then he would elaborate even more.

We both had a great eye and helped each other with no video cameras, only each other to refine the golf swing he was teaching me that we both believed in. It made perfect sense to me to develop my golf swing in his image since there was no one around pure as Moe.

There was good conversation in between shots since we both were enthusiastic to hit the golf ball even better for the next time. Moe was a pleasure to watch and he also enjoyed how I was progressing from his teaching. We talked about his meeting with Irv Sloch and Moe showed me the new xx shafts that the club repair man added to his clubs. Moe decided to put a little clinic on for me and hit three or four drivers off the fairway. I was amazed at how solid the golf ball flew like an arrow with a slightly lower trajectory than if he used a tee. Moe told me that it was a handy shot to have in case he couldn't get home with a three wood on a par five. When we approached the green Moe said, "Greg, how is your bunker play?"

Moe dropped a dozen balls in the bunker and hit every shot within six feet making it look so natural and simple. Moe would say, "I spank the ball as if I was hitting a board buried in the sand shallow and never get too deep. The sand iron is for bunker shots and sometimes out of heavy rough around the green. I use my pitching wedge for other shots under a hundred yards."

I hit bunker shots attempting the same technique. I did pretty good but my sand iron didn't have a big enough flange to spank it properly. The parking lot was close so Moe took a quick walk to his car and returned with a big flanged sand iron similar to his.

Moe handed me the sand iron and said, "Here you go pal, you can have this one. Now work hard and get used to it for next time we play." I thanked Moe and told him I would practice hard. After all these years I still have the same big flanged sand iron in my bag.

I would soon head home to Toronto, Canada, to start my apprentice-ship as an assistant professional at the Weston Golf Club under head professional Gordon Delaat. Weston Golf Club was an older style golf course where Arnold Palmer won the Canadian Open in 1955.

The best score I shot my first winter down south was a smooth 70 but believed I might have done better if my course management improved even though my tee to green game was good. Moe would say, "A walk in the park."

Before my flight departure, I thanked Lawson Mitchell for his exceptional Hospitality. We shook hands with an invitation to return next winter. Moe already knew I was leaving and would see me back in Toronto at the Pleasure Park driving range around April 15, after his stop in Augusta at the Masters.

He attended every year on his drive home to Canada, where we would continue our golf relationship.

Moe was invited to the Masters in 1956 and 1957 as the 1955 and 1956 Canadian Amateur Champion and hit the majority of fairways and greens respectively.

It was unfortunate that he had trouble with the greens coming from snow country directly to play in a world class event. His ball striking was unbelievable and it would be safe to say from tee to green he out classed the best in the world. Moe always returned to watch the practice rounds and associate with the participating professionals that knew Moe and respected his talent for striking the golf ball.

Each year Moe would leave directly from Florida to make his appearance at the Masters tournament that he experienced as a player with many memories close to him. Once I was back in Toronto I would look forward to spending the 1975 summer practicing and playing with my new friend. Moe was a master ball striker with a ton of incredible golf knowledge that he generously made available to me.

Greg Lavern and Moe Norman

Golf Haven G.C. just north of Toronto years later in 1981. Our golf relationship and friendship was ongoing throughout the seventies and eighties. Moe had his favorite outfit on, brown shoes, red pants and black turtle neck. I kept this picture close to me for many years and it reminded me of the great memories and opportunity to learn the golf swing from the greatest ball striker in the world.

Ben Hogan welcomes Hogan Staff Professional Lawson Mitchell in 1970

This was the Sand Iron Moe gave me in the seventies to improve my Bunker game. I still use the same Sandy today and never changed. The big flange made bunker play much easier and felt natural to me.

Chapter 2 –
Practice and Play with Moe in Canada

It was April 15, 1975, after my first winter with Moe. I decided to check Pleasure Park Driving Range out in my 1970 Chevy Nova to see if my buddy was back in Canada. I walked in the entrance and Moe was sitting on the bench inside the pro shop reading the same book he had down south with his favorite driver in hand. Moe looked up, "Hi pal, you made it back."

"How was your trip Moe?"

"Driving was good with a stop off at the Masters and now back home ready to play when the courses open here."

"We will have to play a bunch of golf this summer when I am not working at Weston G.C."

Moe stood up and said, "Let's hit some now, I have nothing to do this morning." We grabbed a couple of large baskets of balls and headed to the far end of the range. The grassy area was still soft and muddy in April. Moe wanted to show me how he was hitting the ball since the last time we played together down south. Some things never change as I watched Moe strike four balls like an arrow with his driver while he chuckled and smiled. "Nothing has changed except I feel lower through the hitting area, my divots are way passed the ball, just bacon strips with the irons and no chance for hamburgers and great flight with the driver."

Moe hit every drive over the 250 yard sign that clearly indicated he put a few more yards that had great flight with the driver he was swinging. Moe had a graphite shaft put into one of the driver heads he liked for a few extra yards. He wanted to get home on some of the longer par fives he would not normally reach in two shots with use of technology rather than altering his swing.

Moe said, "Feels good though I prefer steel, just have to get my timing with the lighter shaft." Moe was giving new technology a try to see if there was any advantage without compromising straightness for distance.

It was really noticeable that Moe's right foot was staying down through the hitting area for a much lower club path into the ball at impact and beyond. "Moe, your much lower through the ball and your right instep is really going down." Moe quickly responded, "My right side is really bowed the same way when I was a teenager. My right leg almost was touching the ground coming into the ball, more push off the right foot and the left knee is pulling and leading for great separation of the legs." Moe continued with a private golf clinic for me to watch and learn. He hit every shot right on the nose, dead straight as his reputation of owning his own swing was skillfully demonstrated. I believe he hit one or two a little right of his intended target. This goes to show that even a great ball striker as Moe Norman can hit a stray one. I asked Moe the feeling he had towards the two stray ones he hit? Moe answered me by saying, "I am only human but the closest to a well oiled machine, usually timing or maybe a little movement. My preference is the ball to move to the right on a bad one and eliminate the left side of the golf course." The funny thing is Moe's bad shots are like most tour professional's good ones that move ten to fifteen yards off line.

Moe wanted to watch me after he polished off his bucket and was pleased that I never changed from the swing movements he was teaching me. We worked on some little things to make my action solid and more the same (MOS).

Moe wanted consistent ball position with my driver inside of the left thigh or heel while teed at normal height for a consistent strike. We then went over to the grass area where Moe wanted me to hit the ball off a normal tee. Moe explained, "Find a consistent height to tee the ball for tournament play; that will provide a better chance to have solid contact in the middle of the club face." When you are hitting your positions there are only little things that can improve solid contact. Moe was like a sly fox when it came to the golf swing. It was incredible the little adjustments he made that affected the more important things with his keen eye.

The rain started to come down, so we headed inside to see Chris Knill, the golf professional and manager of the range. Chris was a jolly English fellow who made his way back from his winter home in Florida at the Sugar Mill G.C. Chris was in good spirits and excited to have the range ready for summer golf.

Chris said, "How are you guys doing?" Chris knew of our close golf relationship and never charged either one of us when we hit balls at Pleasure Park. Chris would say when we offered to pay him, "You guys are always good for business when you are here." If we had the urge to hit a lot of balls we would pick them up to help save Chris on labor costs with the range picker.

Inside the golf shop six regular customers usually sat around telling golf stories while hanging around waiting for Moe to open up his colorful world of golf to them. It was like old home week usually Saturday morning or the odd evening through the week. Moe was in his comfort zone from the friendly surroundings that allowed him to be his happy go-lucky self. Moe was usually shy if he entered unfamiliar surroundings. He required myself or someone in his inner circle to introduce him or he would just walk away. Moe had two inner circles: the friends he knew, and the ones he really trusted and wanted to be around. Trust and integrity were important with Moe when he self-evaluated the characteristics of a person after a recommendation was made for association. Moe would treat the majority of people with respect unless you were someone that caused problems while he was occupied or minding his own business. Of course there were people with the intention to cause a disturbance out of jealousy or to provoke a situation rather than give praise and encouragement.

I can remember a few times I had to intervene when Moe was terribly provoked to actually save the fellow from the hand of Moe. His hands were strong like a vise and particularly his left hand where you would not get away. I used to tell Moe that these trouble makers were not in his league and not to go down to their level. Regardless of the situation good, bad or the ugly, we faced it faithfully together despite the outcome.

It was the summer of 1975 and our normal routine consisted of travel from Pleasure Park to Golf Haven Golf Course to practice and play nine holes. We would privately golf in Canada throughout the seventies and early eighties each summer. I would meet Moe at Pleasure Park and together we proceeded up the highway to Moe's home course, Golf Haven G.C. When driving in his blue Cadillac we would listen to motivational tapes of the golf teachers that taught the golf mind during the seventies. Paul Bertholy, Bob Toski and Irv Slosh inspired Moe with knowledge on the mind, but he wasn't interested in their views on mechanics.

It was our first trip to Golf Haven Golf Course where Moe had dressed for the occasion with the same outfit consisting of brown shoes, red slacks and black turtle neck that he wore when we were first introduced. Moe always was sentimental and would dress for an occasion in appreciation toward someone or a particular tournament he previously won. There was one outfit I liked from Moe's wardrobe that looked very professional on him. It was his black leather Foot joy shoes, light blue slacks and white shirt with red dots. Moe was a flashy dresser even though he didn't coordinate all the time. When I look back in time Moe dressed for himself, not the public, and dressed with bright colors depending on his mood. One thing for sure Moe wore the best of quality in golf wear and it was always a surprise to see the colors he attempted to coordinate.

When Moe opened the trunk of his car, it look like a miniature pro shop on wheels with balls, accessories, shoes, drivers and sets of irons. The practice balls we would be hitting were all Titleists, slightly used, in a large bowling bag that held around eight or nine hundred balls. It was important to have the same feel during practice or on the golf course. We use to have contests making the smallest pile we could, and Moe would always win. It was fun trying to equal him; that made me strike it great when considering I was hitting shots with the world's best.

Moe would say, "Make your pile smaller. The smaller the pile, the better you strike it that day."

While hitting about 400 balls before going out to play I was given some special insight from Moe on the range. I was athletic and strong and progressed quickly with Moe's secrets during the summer months.

Moe would say, "What goes up must come down." Moe referred to the left shoulder generating upward as the right side drives down. This is a key component in building a pendulum swing that is the closest to a prefect golf swing. Each ball Moe struck was in machine like fashion, as if you pressed a button. Moe made it look that simple. Moe told me, "I never let the golf ball control me, I control the golf ball." I told Moe that I loved his trajectory and soft landing. He grinned at me and then whispered in my ear, so no one else could hear his words of wisdom, "Flight tells all." Moe could tell the purity of the golf shot from its flight.

It was a sunny afternoon after our morning practice with the desire to bring our good shots to the first tee. Moe would say, "Now we take the longest walk in golf the same way champions do." Just before we teed off Moe reminded me to continue hitting my positions without hesitation with good visualization on my target. Moe said, "This is what golfers forget to do when they leave the practice tee. Losers allow the golf ball to control them; champions control the golf ball."

Our three or four drives off the first tee all found the middle of the fairway. We walked together, joking in leisure between shots. Moe liked to wrap his shafts half way down with black and red Goodwin wrap on grips while approaching his shot. I had a similar set Moe gave me where we both would wrap hockey tape securing the bottom of the grip. The wrap-on-grip had exceptional feel and it was unfortunate the rubber factory in Kitchener, Canada, stopped production and then quickly became non-existent. Once our grips were wrapped we arrived at our centered drives and it was down to business with total concentration on hitting beyond the flag. Moe blurted while in motion, "Like that, aim over the flag."

Moe continued, "I usually take one more club and choke down on the grip with space behind the flag to spin it back a foot or so. I give myself two chances to hole my shot." The flag was soon surrounded with a swarm of golf balls. Moe, the competitive sportsman, said, "Your turn pal to make a birdie out of the gate."

I did what Moe told me and made two birdies and two pars. Moe had made four birdies out of four balls. Score only counts in tournaments though sometimes we played total score with four balls or worst ball using two balls for consistency.

After playing about six or seven holes Moe said, "Got to do something, be right back." I figured nature was calling but Moe had some other business to take care of. On his quick return Moe showed me a roll of bills that consisted of eight or ten thousand dollars. That was a lot of money in our day. I just stood watching with my mouth open. Moe said, "I needed some spending money; now I am back."

Moe did not believe in banks and had money hidden in secret places on different golf courses known only to him. Moe put the roll of bills in his pocket and continued as if nothing happened after an unexpected hilarious laugh from my buddy who never ceases to amaze me.

Moe told me that a par three was playing about 165 to the flag downwind. I can remember he hit seven iron with two balls since he normally hits his 7 iron 145 yards under normal conditions. I had selected a 6 iron since I was gripping down an inch or so from my previous tip from Moe earlier on the practice tee. I hit two balls with pretty attractive flight. Moe turned to me and looked me straight in the eye. Moe said, "Do you realize what you just did to hit it on the green, do you know what you got?" I was not sure just what Moe was saying, but soon found out how strong he was when he wrapped his arms around me and gave me a big bear hug.

With a lot of emotion Moe said, "That is a sign of greatness, Greg old buddy, you drew both balls back five feet down wind like me when I was setting course records." Moe identified my fresh ball marks when we arrived at the putting surface and just shook his head.

Moe was still shaking his head with amazement all the way to the 9th hole since he witnessed something different, unusual, and similar to his own talent and ability. When we finished, he turned to me again and said, "Do you know what you did out there? I thought I was the only one that could suck it back down wind." I thanked Moe for his awesome help on gripping down for control and told him it felt like the ball was stuck to the face.

After the round we stopped in to say hello to the owner of Golf Haven who knew Moe had taken me under his wing for practice and play at his facility.

Moe in a fine sitting position with his weight on his heels.

Moe wanted his right leg and instep to work downward.

I knew Ed Membery from Tomoka Oaks. Lawson Mitchell had previously introduced me while in Ormond Beach. Ed Membery, confined to a wheel-chair, was a gentleman with good business sense who helped Moe with finance planning. Ed gave Moe a place to practice and play and encouraged him to compete on the Peter Jackson Canadian Tour. In return Moe would represent the golf club and promote junior golf. I shook hands with Ed Membery when he told me I was welcome anytime I was with Moe. On our departure we grabbed a couple of Cokes from the Coke machine for our drive back to Pleasure Park.

Moe put on some soft relaxing music as we headed down the highway. Moe told me, "When you drive to a golf tournament, play soft music that will relax your mind to keep you patient and not anxious." Moe put on one of his motivational tapes in his tape deck that talked about the importance of getting your mind conditioned before you start your round of golf. Moe dropped me off at my car after an awesome day of practice and play where the same routine continued for many more summers in Canada. I thanked Moe and told him it was my pleasure. Moe responded by saying, "It was my pleasure old buddy, my pleasure."

Chapter 3 –
Back to Ormond Beach Florida
with Moe and Lawson

The summer came to a close for practice and play with Moe who left for Florida in late October while I was still working at Weston G.C. until November. Moe knew I would be down and told me to check at the golf club for his whereabouts. This trip I decided to drive in my green 1970 Chevy Nova that would be my reliable transportation back and forth to the golf courses in the area. My drive down was enjoyable stopping at the trucker stops to rest and eat. Once I arrived there were few changes from my first experience with Moe and Lawson. I knew Lawson had made a career change from Tomoka Oaks to Director of Golf at The Club at Indigo.

When I arrived at the new facility just down from the speedway Lawson welcomed me with direction that I would be staying at his dad's place for the winter rather than Ryles Inn.

I was informed that Moe had moved down to a new golf course called Spruce Creek G.C. After our introduction and a few laughs we drove out together in a golf cart to meet Bill Mitchell who was the greens superintendent and a life member of the Canadian and United States Professional Golfers Association.

Bill Mitchell was a very talented man who played both golf and hockey really well. In his early years as an assistant professional he worked for Head Professional Lloyd Tucker at Rock Way Golf Club in Kitchener. Both Lloyd and Bill played a great part in Moe Norman's early development.

Moe always trusted and respected Bill who was Moe's watchful eye in Canada and future years when Moe spent his winters at Tomoka Oaks. Moe would listen to Bill who provided the best of advice when asked or required. Besides the life experiences, Moe was also provided with basic fundamentals in those early years and never did Lloyd Tucker or Bill tamper with his approach. Both men knew a young Moe would one day become the greatest ball striker the world has ever seen. Bill was certainly a major player in Moe's inner circle of friends while Moe was developing his talent.

Bill played professional hockey in the National Hockey League when it was only a six team league with the Chicago Black Hawks. Bill played defense dropping his gloves with the best of them. Moe and Bill had a friendship that flourished over the years as great sportsman.

The first thing Bill said to me was, "The door is open make yourself at home. You look like a young Moe and probably eat like him. Hope you can do dishes." Bill was a tough straight shooter and if you were respectful he would be great to you, as was my experience. Before I left to get settled after my drive down, Bill said, "We will have lots to talk about over the winter. Just ask. I will be home once I finish at the golf club for the day." Lawson took me back to the pro shop and gave me directions to his dad's place. During the winter Bill knew I spent my days playing or practicing with Moe, which he highly encouraged.

There were some times I played golf with Bill at The Club at Indigo, and he helped me with my putting. Bill passed on some great information after collaborating with Lawson who was a solid putter with a good short game. His left hand was the leader on the putting stroke or chipping motion. Lawson and I had the knowledge of left hand dominance that Dave Stockton promoted to tour players that are winning professional golf tournaments years later.

Bill and I spent many hours in the evening watching old black and white films of Moe. I remember those evenings when Bill would haul out his reel projector in total darkness to view Moe. Time with Bill was most enjoyable, with his hospitality and knowledge that he passed on that provided more understanding of Moe as a person and also knowledge about myself. Bill knew I could swing like Moe with encouragement to never change from the golf swing Moe was teaching me. I would later thank Bill for his friendship and everything he shared with me.

After getting introduced to my accommodations for the winter, my evening would involve some great conversation as Bill went through his life experiences.

Bill knew Gordon Delatt, the head professional I worked for in Canada who spoke very highly of him. I gave Bill some of my golf background while we talked until it was bedtime. Of course Moe was the topic of conversation with focus on what really happened to Moe while growing up. Moe had it rough and was very poor until he got a few bucks in his pocket when he turned professional. No one worked harder than Moe Norman day in and day out as many would agree.

Of course this first night was a brief overview over three or four hours and Bill continued to educate me with all sorts of understanding and truth of Moe's early years. This time frame I was unfamiliar with since I was introduced to Moe during the winter of 1974 when we started our golfing relationship. After our talk I was eager to hunt Moe down tomorrow at Spruce Creek G.C. Bill knew Moe would be surprised and excited that I was here to play with him all winter. Bill said, "Get to bed; you want to be sharp for Moe."

In the morning I called Spruce Creek pro shop. When a lady answered, I requested that Moe come to the phone. "Tell Moe it is Greg and I just got down from Canada." Moe happened to be standing in the pro shop and he took the phone. Moe said, "Hi old buddy. I am playing at Spruce Creek now. Get over here I will wait for you. It's a nice day." I told Moe I was staying with Bill Mitchell, but would leave now for Spruce Creek. Moe said, "See you soon pal." It was the first time we talked on the phone, much different from the face to face appointments we normally made. Many have said over the years that Moe will only talk on the phone if he knows you or trusts you. Moe went to the phone immediately when he knew I was calling. He spoke clearly though I sensed a little shyness as if talking on the telephone was something he didn't do very often.

When I walked in the pro shop Moe shook my hand and said, "Great to see you old buddy, now it's time to work." I showed my CPGA card though Moe had already made arrangements with the golf course to play with him all winter.

The golf course had just opened, and there were many golfers the first year. It was a great opportunity to hit four balls a hole that Moe and myself liked to do when playing golf we would play at Spruce Creek and practice at the speedway grass parking lot with Moe's big bag of balls. That was great for practice — to hit and pick up our own balls.

We continued summer golf in Canada to winter golf in Florida through the seventies and early eighties, year after year. Moe committed himself for many years at Tomoka Oaks until Lawson resigned to further his career as Director of Golf at the Club at Indigo. Moe would play with Bill and Lawson when invited, though the majority of time was spent at Spruce Creek G.C. Moe and I would play through the week at late afternoon or practice at the speedway mid-morning. It was essential we combined practice and play for performance.

Moe never changed just to satisfy the millions of golfers that have been brainwashed by style or the classical pretty swing. Moe's way of thinking was to have a swing that produces solid effective results every day. Moe taught me to use one waggle and pull the trigger with smooth centrifugal force. Moe would say, "My golf shots become attached to me."

Moe did not play golf without thinking and understanding his surroundings. Make no mistake; playing fast had nothing to do with not thinking or blanking your mind. Moe would put his mind to use twenty yards before he would hit the shot. Moe, the leader of fast play, set the example for the rest of world to follow!

Once Moe was into his set-up, he started his swing motion usually by maintaining one key thought. When his singular thought was clear, Moe's swing followed a pattern for a consistent solid strike. Moe would insist to let it happen and trusted his positions when he attempted to hit.

Moe would often say, "A pretty swing means nothing; hit your positions." If you hit it with your practice swing, then you will never hit the golf ball pure. Moe never took a practice swing when playing a round of golf. The only time was when he demonstrated positions of his pure move.

Why would someone trust a practice swing rather than pull the trigger with effectiveness?

Why do you think Moe never took a practice swing? Simple, it only counts when a golf ball is launched.

Great players have to hit lots of balls to develop a repetitive swing. It does not count if you swing in the air or grace the grass. Besides, your practice swing is difficult to reproduce on the course for two reasons: there is no key thought, and no focus on your target. Therefore it is useless. If a practice swing makes one feel better before the actual strike, then understand the purpose of the practice swing which is to develop better feel. George Knudson used to practice with his eyes closed to feel the swing motion without distraction. He got so good at it that he could actually hit the ball with closed eyes since the ball was just getting in the way of the club face through impact.

Moe had such a great feel to where the practice swing for him was a waste of time.

Moe would say, "If you miss it, then miss it quick, this is a game of misses with nothing wrong with a frozen rope or a missed straight shot on the fairway."

Spruce Creek was a good challenge for Moe, and he spoke highly of the golf course to people that asked where he was playing. Smaller greens and a great indentation from tee to green along the fairway edge for a good target on tee shots. I gained important knowledge from Moe with a great opportunity to manufacture his unique golf swing while playing three or four balls a hole. There was a special concentration on course management that Moe would include in his teachings while walking up the fairway.

Moe and I continued to practice or play together using the same old routine morning till dusk for the winter. It would be golf all day and dinner at Morrison's unless Bill told me before hand that he wanted to prepare supper. Bill was a meat and potato guy who could make a stew that tasted great after a long day at the golf course. Moe came over to Bill's a few times with me for stew night. After we ate then it was conversation for a few hours. Bill and Moe had lots of stories that kept me entertained. I just listened while many good old memories of a young Moe Norman were brought to life.

One story I recall on the hottest day of the summer when Moe decided to practice at Rockway G.C. Moe hit over a thousand balls that particular day when the rest of the membership was finding shade to stay cool.

Moe entered the pro shop while Lloyd Tucker and Bill Mitchell were standing by the golf shop counter. Moe's hands were full of blood and his clothing was soaked to the bone as if he was swimming. Moe used to run up a steep hill at the club with his golf bag over his shoulder to strengthen his legs. Bill said, "Moe you were a great back then becoming one of the greatest leg players in the game." Moe worked very hard on his swing in those days over a five year period.

There was great fun when Moe and Bill got together, but it was no laughing matter when rehashing the hard times. Moe went through many struggles in those days with only a chocolate bar and Coke for lunch. Any money Moe came into from caddying and pin setting was for tournament expenses and entry fees. Moe had holes in his sneakers when going to amateur tournaments.

When Moe started to make money in the professional ranks he was fashioned with the best golf shoes money could buy. This was a reminder to Moe of the hard times he experienced during the "dirty thirties" while dedicated to the game he loved. Bill watched over Moe during the early years, and the respect Moe showed Bill later in life was clearly demonstrated when they spoke or played golf together.

Christmas in Ormond Beach usually involved drinks of cheer with conversation. Floridian Christmas would still allow a round of golf during the morning before the festivities of family or friends got started.

Together we played golf in the morning before we headed out for Christmas dinner. I gave Moe his present and he had one on hand for me.

It was funny that we both purchased golf socks. Moe said, "Great minds think alike."

Lawson, Bill and I became Moe's close true friends during the winter time. Moe was invited to either Lawson or Bill's house for Christmas dinner for which he always showed up. I told Moe I would be having turkey with Bill since he would have dinner prepared. Moe said, "Going to Lawson's to eat, play with the kids."

I told Moe to enjoy himself when I wished Moe a Merry Christmas. Moe said, "Pal, you're always at the top on my list." Thanks Moe for your words and present.

After Christmas I headed down to Spruce Creek to meet Moe and see if play or practice was on his agenda this week. Moe wanted to head to the Speedway for practice in the grass parking lot. Moe was excited since he viewed himself on the projector from a film Lawson had previously taken and loved what he saw.

Moe said, "Old buddy, I want to hit some balls pal and show you myself what I used to do so well." In a flash, Moe would demonstrate while I watched with excitement. Moe would not tell me at first since he wanted to provide the opportunity for me to pick out his new insight and see how smart I was. After a few attempts Moe would tease me with a whisper of his confidential information for my ears only. Moe noticed he was more centered in relation to the golf ball on the downswing from the 1963-64 films he viewed. Moe not only told me of his new awareness but the actual move or how he performed the actual move.

The golf swing Moe was teaching me was the same as the pictures taken from an 8mm camera by Lawson. There are none like them in the world. This is the same swing Moe used to win the 1955 and 1956 Canadian Amateur Championships and the 1974 CPGA Championship the first summer I was with Moe in Canada.

Moe showed an interest toward Paul Bertholy and asked Lawson Mitchell to call him so that he could visit after the Masters on his way home to Canada in April of 1975.

Around February during the winter of 1976 Moe asked me if I would go for a drive with him to visit Paul Bertholy I told Moe I would gladly drive up with him. We left in Moe's car from Ormond Beach, Florida, and headed to Foxfire G.C. in North Carolina. Paul Bertholy welcomed us at the door and had breakfast ready. Moe said to Bertholy, "I brought my pal Greg. Hope you don't mind." Paul Bertholy shook hands with me and said, "You are one lucky fellow, Gregory, to have the opportunity to practice and play golf with the straightest striker in the world. Learn everything you can as your knowledge will be required by many."

After breakfast we hit some balls on a mild day that was unusual for February in North Carolina. I didn't think we would be able to hit balls but gladly hit a few when Paul asked Moe and me to hit some for him. After a few swings Paul said to me, "I can tell from the positions you are hitting that Moe has been teaching you." While Moe was hitting balls, Paul showed his excitement of the effective

rod or lever with the lead arm and how the claw or retained right hand stayed in perfect position for the late hit. Bertholy told me, "Moe has one of the best pre-impact positions as a result of the enormous lag created during the vertical drop or transition."

Paul Bertholy was a PGA teaching professional that distributed his own teaching manual he called <u>The Bertholy Method</u>. The program was structured to train the muscles to react naturally to the desired positions for a repetitive action. The model Bertholy used was Ben Hogan, who was considered a world class striker of the golf ball. Moe could already strike it pure. There was nothing Bertholy could suggest, or he would be messing with true perfection. Moe had a desire to coordinate his mind and ability to strike the golf ball as one, which Bertholy recognized.

Bertholy believed that muscle memory would be achieved when your muscles are trained to hit your positions. He invented a black and red leather wrapped weighted swing pipe. The original Bertholy book was in original green print. I was given both when I showed up with Moe as his student. Bertholy said, "You are the only young professional Moe has ever brought with him. You're special to be so close to Moe, and I see this from how solid you hit it."

I thanked Paul for the items he provided me. In the seventies, Bertholy's manual was only provided to someone that visited him person-ally. Many years later I passed the same book on to a former student I taught named Mike Bourne when spending time in Halifax, Nova Scotia. Mike now resides in the Toronto area and has preserved my original book in plastic over the years.

It would be fair to say that Moe traded services with Bertholy. He would explain the importance of the mind, and in return Moe would hit balls for him since Bertholy understood greatness. Moe was not your normal golf professional; he was in a league of his own. The Bertholy Method provided inspirational direction to reach your potential in the same fashion Ben Hogan and Moe Norman demonstrated their legendary approach toward achievement of the master move.

Paul Bertholy in my opinion was a gentleman with lots of knowledge that I would consider in our era a top world class teacher that presented enlightening seminars in the latter part of his teaching career. Our time together was coming to an end. Moe and I needed to hit the road back to Florida. While we were going out the door, Paul invited me back to his residence on my return home to Canada in April.

Our drive back to Florida was full of conversation about the contents in Paul's manual while we listened to some motivational tapes during the long drive. Moe mentioned, "I liked it when Bertholy said you were hitting it solid and saw my moves in you. I wanted someone else that knew what to look for in the swing besides me." Moe again stressed, "Hit your positions when you practice so they become effortless on the golf course so you are target oriented. Feel you will hit it good every day so your golf shots are part of you." Moe then stopped at his favorite truck stop to grab a quick bite to eat that tied us over while driving until we reached Ormond Beach later that evening.

After Moe and I returned from Foxfire G.C. there was approximately a month left to play golf before I would have to head back to Canada to start the summer golf season. My winter stay was going quickly and March was closing in. During March I practiced daily and spent some time with the Mitchells playing golf. We had some good games that were really competitive.

I recall Lawson shooting many low scores when he played at Tamoka Oaks or The Club at Indigo. Lawson was fairly straight for being a long hitter, and Bill could shoot in the low seventies when his arm wasn't bothering him. There was one round when Moe and Lawson both shot 66 while Bill and myself stayed steady at par enjoying some great shot making from our playing partners.

It was always great to play with knowledgeable players better than yourself for future improvement.

After the golf round we all had a few laughs and the four of us enjoyed the social side of golf where men are gentleman both on and off the golf course. It was clear to me when Moe was around people he enjoyed; his good manners and happy go lucky personality flourished. When Moe was in his comfort zone he was in dynamic form and was certainly exciting to be around. Naturally we marveled how Moe hit the golf ball that made the game look so easy while we valued his friendship even more. Moe knew when he was around people he could trust that no harm would ever come to him. Moe's exciting, enjoyable character could be released.

Moe and I continued to play and practice faithfully throughout the college break at Spruce Creek with practice at the Speedway at the quiet part of the day. We would go where it was the least busy, since Moe did not like crowds, nor did I. One day in March we had just finished hitting Moe's bowling bag of balls and made an unexpected stop at the local corner bar in Ormond Beach. I knew Moe didn't drink but thought he might enjoy the karaoke bar at happy hour.

This was a different experience for Moe, but he was receptive to have a different experience. I told Moe he didn't need to drink, but he could order a Coke and listen. Moe responded, "No beers for me in all these years, maybe it is time to start."

I responded, "NOT TODAY, Coke will be fine. Moe said, "Nope, I am ordering a beer."

Of course Moe was playing. Once we were seated, our waitress asked Moe what he was drinking. Moe ordered a large coke with ice, while I had a large draft. I was not as snow white as Moe but I enjoyed a few beers on a hot day. After a few drafts and seeing Moe was enjoying himself, I told him I was going to get up and sing karaoke. With a chuckle Moe said, "Go for it." I sang a few familiar 50's songs and the crowd all clapped. When I was done, I asked the host entertainer to sing "My Way" by Frank Sinatra for my friend Moe.

Moe had previously told me that "My Way" was his favorite song. As the song was being performed, I could hear Moe humming and his total focus on the words. It was as if he was rehashing the good times and the bad in his life. Moe knew that through it all that he did it Moe's Way. After the song ended I paid for the drinks and we would head out since the second hand smoke was bothering Moe. When we got to the car Moe said, "I enjoyed myself, just the smoke bothered me."

It was a full day of golf practice, karaoke, dinner, watching bowlers, along with a routine drive around the city in Moe's car. Around 10:00 p.m. Moe dropped me at my car to drive back to Bill's residence where I would sleep. I wanted to take advantage of every chance to play or practice since my money was running out and so was my stay. Moe seemed to sense my financial position and made sure we utilized our golf time wisely so I could grasp all I could.

During my final couple of days, before I would drive north to Canada, I stopped at Foxfire G.C. to visit Paul Bertholy as promised. I spent time with Bill and Lawson at Club at Indigo who watched me hit some balls and gave some suggestions that could improve me. I told Bill I would see him before I left since I was sleeping at his house this evening before my drive back home. I told Lawson I would be back next year when Bill mentioned I could stay with him next year.

On my final afternoon in Ormond Beach I went to meet Moe at Spruce Creek where we played nine holes and hit our normal four balls a hole working on shots and did some fine tuning on my swing. Moe liked how solid I was hitting the golf ball and particularly liked the way I was so connected in hitting the positions we spent much time working on over the winter. I learned a few things that day that would remain with me always as part and parcel of the pendulum swing and master move Moe passed on to me. I knew from Moe's expert direction my practice sessions would be worthwhile from practicing the right things for rapid improvement.

Moe hit a few drivers that were so awesome to watch you could have laid a towel over his four balls in the middle of the fairway. It was a great way to end our playing till we continued again in Canada. Together we walked to Moe's car, and he opened up his trunk. Moe said, "I want you to take four drivers back and you keep one yourself to use. Here is $400.00 cash to help get home, you can give me three drivers and the $400.00 back when I see you again in April at Pleasure Park."

"Moe, you don't have to do that."

Moe said, "No problem pal. You have always been honest to me and if I ever had a son I would want him just like you."

"Thank you, Moe. You have been really good to me and I appreciate it."

Moe followed up by saying, "Greg, just hit it pure and don't listen to all the fools out there that only think they know, and know nothing that counts."

This evening would be our last dinner at Morrison's since I was hitting the highway in the morning. I had $400.00 of Moe's money so it was appropriate and proper that I buy dinner. It was a good night for eating from the foods displayed. Both of us hesitated to indulge with two main courses and two deserts. Our stomachs were both slimmed down fairly well from all the balls and playing we did over the winter. Moe was very cautious about his waistline during the era he taught me and certainly was not the size portrayed during the nineties as an older man. Moe went over his swing in detail to make sure I understood everything.

Moe knew his golf moves he wanted me to make better than anyone on this planet. After our conversation I wished Moe the very best until I saw him again.

I confirmed I would stop in to see Bertholy and then meet Moe at Pleasure Park around the middle of April. Moe was excited and pleased that I would be working at the National Golf Club with a fine tour player named Al Balding who Moe respected. Moe with his final words said, "See you soon Greg."

In the morning I thanked Bill Mitchell for his hospitality as I headed to Foxfire G.C. in my 1970 green Chevy Nova. My car was awesome for speed though it was vital I stayed within the speed limit traveling on the US highways. Lawson would always say to me, "Don't hurt your car or your wallet." I did not have extra for any fines and needed my money for gas, food and lodging. I was focused to drive directly to Paul Bertholy's residence and timed it so I would arrive in the early morning.

I was greeted at the door by Paul who said, "Moe's student, glad you stopped by on your way back to Canada." Paul invited me to his table to sit down for breakfast which was good timing. We talked about Moe and Hogan and various sections of his teachings in his manual called The Bertholy Method. There was discussion on the Master Move, the left arm rod and right hand retained claw. I was asked questions on what Moe did, and he provided his perception of the golf swing as Ben Hogan was his model. We were on the same page regarding the similarities between these two great ball strikers.

I mentioned to Paul that I was familiar with some of the terms in his manual from teachings with Moe and the terminology he was using. Moe had told me, "Finesse it and never force the shot, always swing at eighty percent. To *stabilize*: the legs are my stabilizers where I play into my legs.

Energize as the left shoulder goes up and generates while the right side goes down, a result from the vertical drop or transition.

Contain or retain the angle at pre–impact.

Release in front of you down the line way passed the ball, the right hand hits on its own accord as the left maintains its bowed position beyond impact."

Paul followed up by saying, "Greg, you're fortunate to have Moe teaching you to become a fine striker and teacher. Moe was the best I have ever seen to hit the golf ball pure and straight." I told Paul that Moe believes in mass over velocity and wants to feel the club head and know where it was during the swing. We both concentrated on hitting our positions and hit the ball solid with smooth centrifugal force rather than making a pretty golf swing. Paul said, "Amen."

After breakfast Paul demonstrated a workout he does regularly with his swing pipe hitting all the positions explained with illustrations in his manual. It was interesting since Moe hit these same positions years before during his competitive golf career. Paul took a plastic golf ball with a string and pulled the string tight to demonstrate the use of centrifugal force as the ball spun with resistance. Paul said, "When the Master Move is performed by Moe Norman and Ben Hogan it is a fine centrifugal golf swing."

Paul asked me if I knew any drills Moe revealed to me. I told Paul that Moe wanted the butt of the grip to drive down over a fifty cent piece on the ground.

Moe's takeaway was already low and long since you can't get much lower starting with the club head a foot behind the ball. The coin outside his right foot was to develop width while the transition or vertical drop took place. The fifty cent piece was placed approximately two feet to the right of the outside of his right foot while in his wide stance. Moe wanted his shoulders back allowing the legs to lead so the shoulders would never slide forward with the lateral move of his legs.

Greg Lavern (2012 Halifax N.S., Canada)
Moe Norman (1964 Ormond Beach, Florida)

Moe practiced regularly during the early sixties shooting low scores.

I spent the entire morning with Paul who told me, when I was leaving, I was welcome anytime. Paul said, "I learn a great deal off Moe who demonstrates the Master Move so well." In return I thanked Paul for his time and we shook hands.

Driving up the highway toward Toronto, Canada, my mind was clear with many hours to think and ponder the knowledge we exchanged during the enjoyable time spent with Paul Bertholy. I really felt Paul knew many things relating to the Moe Norman or Ben Hogan swing but did not really know the important things I knew from Moe's teachings of how he actually executed his swing. Moe's real desire was to understand Bertholy's approach to the golf mind and develop his vocabulary with big impressive words. Even though Paul Bertholy was a well known golf teacher, he still capitalized on learning from the master ball striker on each yearly visit when Moe would hit balls for him.

Chapter 4 –
Time Spent with Canadian Greats:
Balding, Knudson and Tucker

After my arrival in Toronto Canada I would be preparing to work at the National G.C. under an experienced tournament player on the Canadian and American PGA Tour. After life as a tournament player Al became involved in the conversion of the old Pine Valley G.C. to the National G.C. with new owner Gil Bleckman. It soon gained the reputation as the toughest course in Canada. The golf course was ideal for someone that wanted to become a really good tournament player with a rating of 74 from the back tees. In front of the pro shop was a three level practice tee for daily practice.

Al was tall, slim and wore his hair styled back. In his younger years he was a red head but his hair started to turn white as he aged. He was known as the "silver fox." When breaking into the pro tour truck driving was where he made expense money to support himself in tournament play. He stayed strong, and lean and in shape from his truck driver duties. His golf swing was long and smooth with great rhythm and tempo.

In fact, Al would say to his two assistant professionals, Mike Hogan and myself, "keep the golf swing long so it has a chance to work on the downswing." When Al Balding practiced he displayed great clearance of the left side that allowed him to release the golf club. My new employer won many provincial Canadian tour events. His big win on the American PGA tour was the Mayfair Open.

Al was one tough competitor who scored well hitting the ball solid with total concentration on hitting fairways and greens. From the school of hard knocks he was dedicated to practice and worked hard around the golf club. We never had video in those days but would help each other with minor adjustments to our golf swings. Mike or I could ask Al to take a look at us if we were playing golf or hitting balls with him. Al would be very accommodating, but in return expected our regular hours in the pro shop and to work on whatever changes he thought would help us.

It was never a concern for either of us to combine our club duties with practice or play since both of us would rise early in the morning. Al wanted us to think and eat golf every day during the summer months. His way of thinking as a young player was to learn the game with the opportunity to absorb knowledge from an experienced tour player and play a great golf course at the same time. Being around Al allowed me to familiarize myself the way he swung the golf club and understand how he would manage himself on the golf course. Al knew I did lots of good things in my swing from my teachings from Moe Norman though there were little jewels he could still provide.

Al spent most of his time performing the duties as director of golf or was on the golf course with club members. He always found the time to practice and play as part of the package of being a top notch tour player. Off the golf course he was a good family man with an understanding wife and well-mannered son, which was the other side of the man.

I often wondered why someone had not written a book on Al Balding since he was one of the best players in Canada to ever play the game. I feel it would be a tribute to his accomplishments in golf. There would be an interesting life story of how a truck driver had the determination to win many tournaments in Canada with wins on the American PGA tour.

Many tour players would come up to the National Golf Club to see Al and play the golf course that I had the opportunity to enjoy daily. I can remember Bill Tape and Ben Kern who hung around the club between golf tournaments to practice and play. Bill Tape was short in stature and Ben Kern was tall and lanky, similar to Al Balding. Ben Kern attended the University of New Mexico on a golf scholarship before turning professional. Eventually, Ben Kern took over from Al Balding as Director of Golf at the National G.C. Both Al Balding and Ben Kern are now deceased though during those special years I sure enjoyed my time with these outstanding professionals. These pioneers of the golf industry were well versed in all areas of the golf business and passed on knowledge that would benefit me in future golf years.

While working at the National with Al Balding I continued my strong friendship with my buddy Moe. Near the beginning of the season I provided Moe with the drivers he requested me to bring back for him. I also paid the $400.00 travel money he generously handed to me down south. I would use the driver and sand wedge faithfully on a daily basis for play and practice.

I would use the X shaft persimmon driver for many years until it wore out, though the sandy is still in my bag. Moe was a stickler for playing with good equipment whether old or new as long as it felt good in his hands. It would be tough playing the game if you have no confidence in the clubs you are utilizing to improve or shoot better scores.

I had spent sporadic times during the summer months with Moe that would become more frequent during the latter part of 1976. When the 1977 golf season rolled around, the club professional at Maple Downs G.C., Irv Lightstone, had an opening for an assistant professional. After Irv had some consultation with Al Balding, I was offered the position. I would work as a starter for the members that required lots of good public relations and pro shop work. This was great preparation when I achieved my class A card with hopes of running my own operation. To learn the golf business from various well respected CPGA professionals could only help in the advancement of my golf career. Irv ran a fine operation and served on the Ontario Provincial Board of Directors. Irv played lots of amateur golf with Moe in the early days and with the extremely talented Al Balding years later.

I worked with three other assistant professionals Dave Castellan, Steve Lance and Garry Price. Irv would play golf with us once his membership obligations were completed. Former assistants Ken Venning, Paul Kennedy and friend Paul Hennrick came to play Maple Downs G.C. In short Irv was a supportive professional that took an interest in the assistants that worked for him.

I could play pretty well and earned a third place finish at the Provincial Ontario Assistants Championship. I also played the 1976

Canadian Assistants Championship and represented Ontario. Previously I shot 74 - 64 to win the Toronto Municipal Championship at Humber Valley Golf Club, setting the course record under tough conditions. I was a good ball striker and player that seemed to be a good fit for the Maple Downs membership.

I can recall playing golf with Art Mintz, a real estate developer and Carl Ungerman, the Toronto boxing promoter who certainly bought the fun back into the game along with many other members that were friendly and showed respect for professional status. I even taught a husband and wife that improved so much they invited me to Florida for a few weeks to teach them before I would head to meet Moe at Spruce Creek G.C. for the winter months.

One time I was playing with Dave Castellan and Steve Lance and happened to hit two solid shots on the second par five over water to a railroad tie small green. My 4 wood flew onto the green and into the hole. Of course I never experienced the impressive record Moe had of hole-outs on par threes, fours and fives in tournament play. This accomplishment felt good especially with Moe excited for me when I mentioned the golf hole I scored it on. Now I would have an ace on a par three, two on a par four and a two on a par five, unfortunately not in tournament play. Moe would say to me, "It takes a great shot to hit your target, but luck comes into play if the ball goes in the hole." Moe hit many great shots at his target where some disappeared and others did not.

Probably the most exciting highlight at Maple Downs G.C. was a first and second place finish at the Maple Downs Annual Charity Golf Tournament for Crippled Children. I was fortunate to be invited to tee it up against some regular tour players. Irv wanted me against a strong field that turned out well with two high finishes on two consecutive occasions between 1977 and 1979.

From my strong finishes in this tournament, I had the opportunity to speak with George Knudson who played in the tournament as a gesture of friendship to Irv Lightstone. I was just a young kid, and George showed his classy side to take an interest in me. It was an honor to rub elbows with one of the greatest ball strikers that played the game in both Canada and the United States. My respect was high for George, the same way Moe recognized his talent and ability for hitting a golf ball. We talked for ten or fifteen minutes before dinner was served. I also discovered he was interesting and intelligent to talk to. I expressed to George that I would like to watch him hit balls sometime and mentioned that Moe was teaching me. George told me to drop into the National G.C. where he had been practicing in the early morning.

Normally George would practice at Oakdale Golf Club, his home course when back in Toronto if not playing on tour. George knew I worked for Al Balding last season at the National G.C., and he knew me fairly well. George said, "Be at the practice tee around 7:00 a.m. any day next week, and you can watch me hit some balls if you are quiet."

It was Wednesday morning, my day off from Maple Downs, showing up at 7:00 am. sharp where George was hitting balls at the far end of the practice tee.

I walked up and sat down on a towel to keep me dry from the early morning dew. George looked up and said, "Hi Greg" then put his head back down to practice.

I sat watching George go through his bag hitting draws and fades. He hit the ball beautifully with great flight while I focused a lot on his lower body action that would start with the left knee driving while the golf club was still going back.

There were similarities that all great ball strikers did from transition to impact if you knew what to look for. I remained quiet as a mouse until George had finished his practice session and took in everything I was witness to. George asked me what I learned, and I mentioned about his transition. George told me, "I move my weight to the ball of the left foot, and my right knee drives over the base of the left foot as my power source." I noticed George stood wide the way Moe and Hogan did for a solid foundation. George looked me in the eye and said, "I modeled my swing around Hogan and spent time with him."

George followed up with some more goodies, "I am working on turning my center or chest away from the ball to the right to keep my hands passive while loading." I thanked George for this private session to watch him and learned a great deal from the insight he provided me. George also mentioned, "There is a teacher in Alabama named Ballard who seems to be on the right track and has incorporated some of my swing thoughts in his teaching."

George, out of curiosity, handed me his seven iron and asked me to hit a couple of shots. George simply said, "Greg, you have a ton of natural ability, let it flow." When I hit George's Spalding seven-iron I noticed that the thickness of the grip was really skinny, much different than the built up grips I play with.

I asked George how many layers of tape he used. George replied, "One, I like to feel steel."

We headed to the clubhouse to freshen up after the practice session. In the Washroom, George washed his hands under the cold running water for a long time. He said, "Cold water on the hands feels great after practice." I asked George one last question before I would head back to Maple Downs. I wanted to know while he was in his sitting position on the set up, why his left knee would be bowed out at the target? George, replied, "My left leg is longer than my right."

I shook hands with George and told him I really appreciated the time he spent with me. George said, "It was a blast, Golf Ball." I laughed, "How did you know my famous nickname?" George said, "Talking to Irv. He told me you were dedicated, and the boys started calling you 'Golf Ball' from the amount of golf balls you hit." George thought this was pretty funny. I then asked George his nickname He smiled and said, "Georgie Porgie to my friends. Hope to see you again Golf Ball." I was fortunate enough to cross paths on another occasion with George at the National Golf Club while still employed at Maple Downs G.C.

George Knudson provided me with his approach to striking the golf ball. Ben Hogan once said, "George Knudson has the sweetest swing on tour."

I noticed many things discussed that were Hogan related were easy for me to understand from my golf education with Moe. We were on the same page for George to elaborate at the highest level, while knowing I would grasp with understanding. One of the highlights in George's golf swing that we focused on was how the back swing and leg drive actually connected.

As the club was being turned away by the center in the backswing the leg drive would start with the weight moving to the ball of the left foot.

While the golf club was still going back the lateral leg drive had already started.

This is one of the reasons why George's swing and my own looked shorter from the early transition of weight shift to the left side.

You will find many of the old time great ball strikers did this. The proper sequence of motion takes lots of practice to get your timing though the results are extremely rewarding.

George told me another golden rule during our practice session that I found very useful for my own swing. George said to me, "Golf Ball, never allow the left eye to move past the back of the ball when coming into impact." This eliminated forward movement and insured the hands returned to the starting position in the initial set up with the added lateral weight shift into a sitting position at impact. Both amateur and professional can benefit from this golden swing tip I was privileged to obtain more than thirty years ago.

It was a great opportunity to have worked with George Knudson even though it was not the close relationship I had with Moe Norman.

Between Moe and George, I was among legends consisting of the number one and number two ball strikers to ever come out of Canada that both became internationally known. Two different styles with the same endless love for the game and an incredibly strong work ethic to achieve greatness. In short, George and Moe respected each other especially when the opportunity became available to show recognition for playing or striking the golf ball.

George Knudson retired from tournament golf in the late seventies to open golf schools at Buttonville G.C. and the National G.C. Unfortunately, George was diagnosed with lung cancer in 1988 that spread to his brain and passed away January 24, 1989. It was a sad day for Canadian Golf when a talented man died far too young at age 55. George won the Canadian C.P.G.A. Championship five times with Manitoba and Ontario Open wins three times each. His highest tournament recognition: winning eight times on the US PGA tour. George Knudson will be missed and his ability will be talked about for many years to come as a true pioneer of Canadian Golf.

During the 1977 golf season, Moe and I practiced at Golf Haven G.C. on my day off or late afternoon when I was not scheduled to work at Maple Downs G.C. During our sessions, I was hitting the ball solid and Moe liked what he saw.

One time we headed towards Kitchener on a road trip to visit Moe's first teacher Lloyd Tucker, the former head professional at Rockway G.C.

Moe wanted another pair of eyes that knew the golf swing, and trusted either Lloyd Tucker or Bill Mitchell from his younger years, for additional advice.

Moe wanted me to meet Lloyd the same way he introduced me to Paul Bertholy at his residence when we drove together from Florida to North Carolina as part of his legacy. Lloyd was waiting at his farm residence wearing a Sam Snead styled straw hat and heavy black rimmed glasses. There was a big field available for us to hit balls where Lloyd would watch and observe patiently for two hours.

Before we got down to the actual golf lesson, we talked about the players that played with Moe on a regular basis. Lloyd said, "Moe played with Nick Westlock, Gerry Kesselring and Gary Cowan who became national champions. You needed to be under par to be low man. Playing with better players was the best way to improve. All four were good friends off the course but great competitors when on the golf course."

I found Lloyd an honest man who was soft spoken but willing to speak his mind. Lloyd Tucker's opinion was the same as Paul Bertholy's, "Greg you have a great opportunity to practice and play with Moe. You will learn lots from him. He is the straightest hitter of the golf ball I have ever seen in my entire career." Before Moe and I started to hit balls, I asked Lloyd about his former assistant Bill Mitchell. Lloyd told me that Bill helped Moe out with his swing and stuck up, or looked out, for Moe against bullies at Rockway G.C.

"How has Bill been?"

I remembered Bill playing hockey for the Chicago Black Hawks. He played golf and hockey really well; I intend to stop in to see Bill on my next trip to Ormond Beach, Florida.

Moe hit some irons shots into the field to start things off while Lloyd watched every shot from various angles. He told Moe two things I recall. The first was to move the ball back a few inches in his stance with iron shots and to get his weight between his insteps a little more so he was more centered in his address position. Lloyd made sure that Moe's basics were solid and consistent with the golf swing that he was familiar with during Moe's amateur days. Lloyd said, "Moe sometimes over time your ball position with your irons can creep forward."

Moe made the small but important adjustment that allowed him to stay that fraction longer over the ball through impact.

With the driver Lloyd told Moe, "tee the ball at the same height whatever your preference, lower or higher, and be consistent."

Moe was pleased and continued to hit his remaining shots straight and solid. Lloyd never really fooled around with Moe's swing and mostly concentrated on solid fundamentals. Lloyd was smart enough to know that a player of Moe's caliber who could repeat their swing only requires a small tune up. Good strikers or players usually polish up their basics first and that usually corrects any swing issues. Moe turned to me and said, "Your turn, Lloyd, don't go easy on him." I proceeded to hit seven irons with good tempo and contact while Moe watched a few and left me alone with Lloyd. Moe wanted me to experience a second opinion from his boyhood mentor without influence from Moe himself.

My set-up and the way I moved were clearly noticeable from all the previous time I spent with Moe practicing and playing. The first thing Lloyd wanted me to do was hold on to the club with both hands with authority so the hands stay together.

Lloyd said, "Allow the club to turn away immediately as the center turns to start your backswing. This is what Moe does well." Lloyd said, "You move your legs similar to Moe. I would suggest you start your lateral weight shift a little sooner before the completion of your back swing. Moe spent many hours timing the turning of his shoulders and movement of his legs."

I noticed my divots became narrow bacon strips, and the contact was solid in the middle of the soft blade iron that had an exceptional feel. With the persimmon driver Moe gave me there was an automatic explosion at the ball that fired off the club face with authority. After our session, I thanked Lloyd and appreciated his sound advice. "Greg, glad Moe brought you, nice to see Moe has a good friend, be good to him," replied Lloyd. Moe soon returned from the car after doing some quiet reading and gave thanks to Lloyd for helping us. Lloyd smiled with emotion looking through his thick rimmed glasses with a clear indication of enjoyment seeing his old friend and meeting a new friend.

On our way back to Toronto, Moe asked me if I learned anything new from Lloyd about my golf swing. I told Moe that Lloyd liked my leg action and told me that I move like you. We worked on the same thing you were teaching me to start my lateral move while the club was still going back. Moe replied, "That's good, that's good." I told Moe that Lloyd wanted me to allow the club to turn away when I turn my center on the back swing the way you do.

I was told to stick with what I have and put your wisdom of the golf swing into practice.

Moe then said, "Now you got a second opinion so you know now. Start to believe in yourself. You got a great move through the ball. Lloyd has known my move for years, and if he did not like what he saw he would tell you." "Thanks, Moe for taking me to meet Lloyd Tucker and can't wait to practice tomorrow."

The rest of the summer I played as much as I could with Moe when he was not playing the Canadian Tour. Of course Moe played with some of his other friends when I had to work at Maple Downs, though the reality was many days and hours were spent with me. There were many jealous people in this world that wanted a piece of Moe. They would try to down grade my relationship and valuable exclusive knowledge provided to me by "the master."

Unfortunately, there are people that make false claims to gain fame that Moe certainly was familiar with. Moe knew the knowledge he passed on to me would prevail over people that refuse to accept reality in the golf swing.

For Moe to spend his valuable time and take someone under his wing as I experienced opens up a new outlook on the golf swing beyond anyone else. For example, take the internet junkie that makes the claim

Moe told him the secret to his golf swing at the trunk of his car is a true opportunist and should feel ashamed. I can assure you that Moe would never give up the keys to his golf swing to just anyone and chose me, who practiced regularly with him.

For the longest time I thought people were just negative and foolish. I remember many members of the CPGA would laugh behind Moe's back and make fun of his action during the era he taught me. These same professionals later tried to claim friendship with Moe after screwing him over in earlier years. These few egotistical fools disrespected him as a man and laughed at his unorthodox posture in comparison to their text book set up. It should be understood that Moe's style was natural to him, and anyone willing to make the necessary changes for a solid foundation was far greater than a broken down left wrist set up of the status quo.

I took a different approach when teaching since I knew both methods and gave people a choice. My students could model their swing like George Knudson or Moe Norman. My set-up of course was a model of Moe. Regardless, I was determined to stand with my ass out so the weight was on my heels that George also did in his set up. There was the odd student that attempted Moe's action who became frustrated and went back to their normal way of playing to avoid being heckled.

The quick fix did not require hard practice, and it was easier to say I can't do what Moe does. I knew Moe's golf swing was true greatness with many similarities of the greatest ball strikers. I was alone with Moe against many professionals that looked at his fast play and high hands only to justify their foolish beliefs that no one could swing or move the way Moe does.

Moe said to me many times, "Greg, you and I release in a different way that gives us great control. Lots of pros think they know but know nothing, some good teachers but mostly bad."

During the seventies and eighties, at times I hit the ball terribly but stuck with it from a young age with strong belief and dedication. I figured it like this: for Moe to hit the golf ball this good then he must be doing something the rest of the professionals don't understand. I can assure you at times I hit it so good that Moe would say, "Man, what the hell do you want." I would tease Moe with a smile and respond saying, "Perfectionists like you and me can always get better." Moe would chase me in fun with his driver, "Smart guy, I will show you perfection. I worked at it every day."

It was a great summer, and I had lots to tell Lawson, who was one person Moe did not mind me discussing his golf swing with because he trusted Lawson.

My knowledge from Moe was totally confidential until he passed away and did not want his swing discoveries given to just anyone. I was learning rapidly each day and valuable golf knowledge was added to my teaching credentials. I gained knowledge from professionals like Knudson, Balding, Tucker and Bertholy. Lawson was very knowledge-able, who had great appreciation of Ben Hogan's swing and was a Hogan staff professional.

There were some Canadian pros I was familiar with from my days at Tomoka Oaks that had the same idea to leave the Canadian winter behind. I remember Herb Holzscheiter, Ken Venning, Tommy Trembley, Bobby Breen and Ken Duggan who were good friends of Lawson Mitchell and knew Moe. There was Gus Maue that knew Moe well through his career. Gus didn't play much winter golf spending most of his time at a beach house making himself unavailable.

These were some of the golf professionals that formed Moe's inner circle besides Lawson, Bill or myself that Moe felt comfortable with Herb Holzscheiter who in later years became the head professional at Weston G.C. travelled with Moe on the Canadian tour across Canada. Herb was a great.guy that would shoot from the hip. He was a good player playing as Moe's normal partner in best ball or pro-pro tournaments. During the summer just before heading south, I replaced Herb since due to other obligations when Moe asked me to be his partner at the Bay of Quinte Pro Best Ball. Moe was teaching me on a regular basis and thought it was time I showed my stuff with him. We played fairly well but finished second behind a team that went super low. I am sure Herb would attest to how enjoyable it was to play with Moe in competition especially when he was on the same team. You would never find a more solid and consid-erate partner as Moe. It was an opportunity of a lifetime for Moe to pick me as his partner in competition. Moe even put a sports jacket on for the dinner and presentation where he received many compliments from the other competitors for his classy look.

Usually my routine was working on a repetitive swing and playing a tournament with Moe was a delightful change. When I missed a day of practice or play with Moe because of other obligations, I felt guilty and disappointed. I truly enjoyed my practice sessions and understanding of Moe's incredible ball striking.

It was hard work and understanding that gave back accomplishment and satisfaction of feeling a golf swing that few will experience.

High school letter

A young Greg Lavern graduated high school at Weston C.I. in 1973

I also enjoyed playing golf with the Mitchells: Bill, Lawson and Billy, when not playing golf with Moe.

We had some fun matches with many good golf shots hit. Bill was Lawson's dad, and Billy was his son who was a young junior at the time. Billy had a sister named Missy around his same age who liked to golf. Missy would ride in the cart with Lawson or Grandpa and really enjoyed Moe when he showed up to say hello, bouncing his golf ball on his driver or wedge. Lawson's children, Billy and Missy remembered Moe being good to young juniors and loved to entertain them. Moe felt comfortable with children and knew there would be no harm from them.

I attempted to play or practice every day I could with Moe for the rest of the winter. If Moe was busy and not playing a specific day, I would play golf with Bill or Lawson. For the rest of the winter it was a similar routine of hard practice and hitting a variety of golf shots on the course. It soon would be that time again for Moe and me to head back to Canada. I usually left earlier than Moe but this year I headed back in early April when Moe left for the Masters tournament.

Moe and I would have one more dinner together before it was time to travel. The following morning I said farewell to Bill and Lawson and headed up the highway Toronto bound. There was golf employment waiting for me once I got home with continued practice and play with my buddy Moe Norman.

Chapter 5 –
Moving On With My
C.P.G.A. Class A Status

In 1979 I obtained my Canadian Professional Golfers Association Class "A" card with a new opportunity to work as an associate professional at Silver Springs G.C. in Calgary, Alberta. I was employed by Rick Martison the club professional in March. My stay was short with an offer to operate Trenton G.C for the 1981 golf season. I moved on with more experience particularly in the merchandise side of the business and memories of an enjoyable season working with Brian Bassin, a young assistant who displayed real professionalism. It is my understanding that Brian remained in the golf business and became an established head professional in Calgary, Alberta.

During the 1981 golf season I spent half the season in Trenton and the other half at the Indian Lake G.C. in Chatham, Ontario. I had some employment issues in Trenton and accepted the Indian Lake position for the short term to finish off the season. I certainly did not appreciate a move half way through the season, but I understood the nature of the golf business sometimes was unpredictable. The majority of professionals were fortunate to stay in a head position for years, where I seemed to relocate more than I hoped for. It was easier to stay in the Toronto area as a golf professional and practice and play with Moe. I had knowledge of every area of the golf business with the strong desire to establish a home base for the long term. To be truthful I made some mistakes that I learned from and took the bumps for them.

In 1982 I ended up back in Weston, Ontario where I would base myself while applying for a head professional position and play some tournaments. Of course I would continue my instruction with Moe who was happy and supportive in continuation of our golf relationship. It would be similar to the seventies while learning Moe's golf swing that still remained with me.

There were some local tournaments to play during the Canadian Tour transition with the Ontario Open, Labbats CPGA Championship, or local club events available to enter without having to travel long distances. The CPGA Championship attracted US PGA professionals Ray Floyd, Ben Crenshaw and Dennis Watson along with other International players that participated to represent their respected countries. The home favorites consisted of Moe Norman, George Knudson and Al Balding as Canada's premier representatives in the field. The tournament was played at Cherry Hill G.C. with tough table

top greens and tough pin placements. There were a few top tour stars that voiced their frustration about the pin positions and the six to eight inch rough. It was tough I will admit, though I welcomed the golf course set up Canadian style.

Moe was still teaching me, and the tournament was an opportunity to put my shot making ability on stage. The main objective was to drive the ball on the fairway to open up the green with a desire to hit my iron shots to the flat portion of the green since the pins were placed on slopes. My ball striking the first day was great the first round. I hit the first eight greens, hit the bunker on number nine and managed to get the ball up and down. I opened with a two under 33 that was tied with first round leader, Norm Jarvis, but faltered with a forty on the back nine from a few three putts. My 73 was great under the conditions but an easy 73 from striking it so well. I followed with a 76 in the second round and made the 36 hole cut with 149 that put me one shot behind Moe and ahead of many regular tournament players.

After the first round I was on the practice range with Moe who was excited and wanted to see how I was hitting it and what I was doing right. While we were talking and hitting balls, Ray Floyd got directly behind me with his arms folded and watched me hit balls for about ten minutes.

He never said a word watching one straight shot after another. After Ray Floyd left I asked Moe, why this great was watching me? Moe said, "Keep doing what you are doing and they all will be watching."

In the third round I was paired with Kelly Murray of Vancouver along with an international player from Argentina. While walking up the fairway, Kelly talked to me about how great it was to have Moe teaching me. Kelly knew of Moe's domination on the Canadian tour but never really had the opportunity to talk with him. There were times that Kelly would sit on his bag before a tournament to watch Moe practice with a cooler of Coke on hand when Moe got thirsty. Kelly said, "Few words were exchanged, but I was getting closer to knowing Moe better." Kelly was known as a long driver who respected Moe's ability to strike the golf ball pure on a string. It was quite clear that Moe was teaching me, and Kelly was impressed with a strong desire to learn how Moe Norman could strike it pure and consistently straight. Later, after the third round was finished, at the range I introduced Kelly to Moe and told him we played the third round together.

Moe said, "Sure, sure, I seen him around." When I got Moe aside I told him that Kelly seems dedicated and maybe you could look at him while on tour together. Moe seemed reluctant at first not wanting someone to waste his time. Moe finally came around at one of the tour stops and started to take an interest in Kelly's game. Kelly knew Moe for many years before his Natural Golf involvement. In future years, Kelly played on the Golf Channel's Big Break where he displayed some of Moe's magic out of the bunkers. I enjoyed my short time with Kelly during the 1981 Labatts CPGA Championship and hoped his friendship with Moe made him a better ball striker.

My practice sessions with Moe continued until 1983 when I left for Moose Jaw Saskatchewan after being offered the head professional position at Hillcrest Sports Center. It was a new pro shop facility and challenging link style golf course under a board of directors that would be a new experience. I was to join a team with Barry Heron, the golf chairman, and Ron Graham, the greens superintendent, to implement the golf operation's foundation for future years. Graham could grow grass anywhere and in my opinion was the reason for Hillcrest's lush fairways while Heron had provided productive direction.

My main function was pro shop operation and to service the membership that included green fee players with lessons and clinics. My first assistant, Gerry Hadwin, worked with me to develop a good junior program and inspire the talented juniors to participate in tournaments. Gerry continued his professional career as golf teacher in British Columbia in later years. Gerry's son, Adam Hadwin, became a fine Canadian player with great showings as low Canadian in the Canadian Open and recently played four rounds in the US Open. There is no doubt Gerry provided some of his understanding of the golf swing that influenced and kept Adam on the right path to the highest stage in Golf. Congratulations Gerry, to you and your son.

I played with three left-handed juniors in the Saskatchewan pro-junior and won the event with team members Kelly Hicke, Ted Tilbury and Brent Kemple who gave the junior program a great start. Ted is now a professional therapist in Vancouver, and Brett took up a professional business career living in Regina, Saskatchewan. Kelly Hicke stayed with competitive golf and accepted a golf scholarship in Texas after junior golf. While attending college, Kelly had a few lessons from Harvey Penick the legendary teacher who taught Ben Crenshaw and Tom Kite. Kelly states, "The connection became possible for me since Moe had taught Greg Lavern in the seventies and Moe was friends with Harvey." Kelly is now a member of the North Texas PGA and owner operator of his own golf sales enterprise.

I enjoyed helping my assistants and talented juniors become better ball strikers to reach their potential. Moe was a great inspiration to me who believed juniors were golf's future. I never forgot how enthusiastic Moe became during the ball striking clinics when he demonstrated for juniors. He always had a few golf balls in his pocket for a little boy or girl that was watching the clinic with amazement.

Moe Norman

Greg Lavern

Moe taught me at a young age to have confidence in myself on the golf course. Walk the walk and do the talk to the beat of your own drummer.

Moe enjoyed children and felt safe around them especially if dedication was displayed at a young age. To watch young golfers progress in golf tournaments and mature throughout life brings joy and great satisfaction of giving back to the game. Moe knew this and was a contributor to junior development.

After a few seasons in Moose Jaw, I had an unexpected visit from Moe on his way to Calgary to play a tournament. We spent the entire day working on the golf swing that brought back many memories from the past. After our introductions and chatting for a little while, we jumped into a cart to play a few holes on the back nine. On the tenth hole, Moe hit three balls from an elevated tee just in front of the green all within a few yards of each other. Moe said, "I am ready for Calgary G.C. Let me at them." Moe told me some of the things he was working on and provided some advice on the golf swing from his past teachings as a refresher. We laughed and joked and would needle each other while striking the ball on the back nine. Moe was in his comfort zone in a relaxed mood when we played together and that brought out his best shots. Moe won the tournament in Calgary. When Moe wanted to win, he could. Our friendship consisted of two dedicated professionals that shared and refreshed a golf swing we believed in.

Chapter 6 –
Attending University: Moe Surprises Me with a Visit

I stayed in Moose Jaw for a few years after my contract ended at the Hillcrest Sports Center and operated the local driving range as a class A professional. There were no available club jobs in the area, so I took my CPGA credentials to the East Coast. In 1989 I was accepted at the University of Prince Edward Island. I was also father to three daughters named Heather, Chelsey and Jerica.

If there would have been another club job in Saskatchewan, I would have remained and not attended University. Funny how one change or opportunity in a different direction can dictate the course of your life or how it might have been. For now it was four years of study and assignments to achieve a degree that should stand out on a resume when applying for my next club destination.

While attending University, the Belvedere G.C. was within walking distance. That was great for my golf game after classes or on weekends. Belvedere was an older style course with small sloppy greens that demanded accuracy, especially when the wind blew. This tight challenging course was the home of Lori Kane, LPGA tour star who won several times during her career on the US tour.

I can recall when Moe gave Lori some advice on her swing. While on tour she praised Moe for how he helped her.

One sunny afternoon in late September 1992, after hitting balls, I was wiping my brow from sweat and drinking a Coke when my old buddy Moe Norman casually walked up behind me. Moe said, "Get to work on what I taught you." It was freaky; there was colorful Moe with a big smile. We shook hands and embraced each other as close friends would that were away from each other for awhile.

I asked Moe, "What are you doing way out here in Prince Edward Island?"

Moe said, "Came to see you old buddy, just stopped in before I head to New Brunswick to do a clinic."

"Moe, how have you been doing with yourself?"

Moe said, "Great, I like doing clinics and hit shots for people." I asked Moe if he would watch me hit a few balls and give me a few things to work on. Moe replied, " I like what you are doing just the way I taught you."

"I never changed Moe, I have been working on that key secret you told me about in your swing and have told no one in all these years since that day in the early eighties at Golf Haven G.C when you put the icing on the cake." Moe watched me hit a few more and said, "Pal, I see you're doing it now. Look at the bacon strips. Flight tells all, and you know how to get it."

It was a warm day, so we walked over to the machine to get a couple of Cokes while catching up on old times about doing clinics for Natural Golf. I asked Moe how he liked doing the clinics. Moe said, "Great, old buddy, I get to show my stuff. Lots of people have never seen a golf ball hit with real purity."

"Moe you taught me your golf swing for years, and it is much different than the Natural Golf Method." Moe said, "I just changed a few things that they wanted me to do for money."

"Moe you taught me left side control and the overlap grip and not the hammer or right side junk. We both know that the right side hits on its own accord way late in the pendulum swing."

Moe replied with a chuckle, "Old buddy you know what I do; others only think they know."

I confirmed with Lawson Mitchell who also had a conversation with Moe in Florida during the late nineties. When he asked Moe if he told anyone about his actual golf swing other than Greg and myself, Moe answered, "Nope, no one but you guys, no one else asked and I was not talking." From both our conversations with Moe it was clear to me that

Moe told no one the important stuff in his golf swing. I strongly believe this since Moe was straight and honest with both of us. It was clear to me that the promoters of Moe Norman never came out with the things I know after all these years. These promoters were grasping at straws and resorted to their own observations.

Moe asked me on our way back from the Coke machine to the range, "Greg when are you done with University?" I told Moe graduation was May 1993, if I maintained my marks. When we arrived back to the practice tee, Moe put his arm around me and said, "When you finish school you will be able to write a book on everything I taught you old buddy."

"Thanks Moe, I will do my best." Moe joked and said, "Just wait till I am six feet under playing with George Knudson on the fairways of heaven."

Moe followed up by saying, "Old buddy, you swing like me and have all my knowledge. Thanks pal for your friendship and dedication to learn."

I told Moe with a tear in my eye that I will never forget the knowledge he gave me and the thousands of balls we hit together. All the sweat and dripping blood we experienced hitting balls together would make the book special or worthwhile as a tribute toward your legacy."

Moe said, "I told you everything I know. Hope you write one someday."

It was getting late, Moe had spent a few hours with me, and it was time for him to drive toward New Brunswick to perform his clinic. I expressed to Moe that we live so far away and we're not likely to see each other again.

Gosh, I missed those glorious days of playing golf together.

Moe put his arm around my neck, "Old buddy I am always with you. See you pal."

I shook hands and then waved to Moe with hope our paths would cross again as I watched him drive away. Moe was off to hit the golf ball better than anyone I had ever seen. My eyes were red from mixed emotions of happiness while memories flashed before me of our incredible golf journey we both treasured.

In 1993 I graduated from University of Prince Edward Island with a good education combined with club professional experience. With the many years I spent learning the golf swing from Moe Norman, I felt I was very qualified to operate a golf facility. I never got the opportunity to put my knowledge and experience into action after I finished my University studies.

After graduation I worked hard on the golf swing Moe taught me during the summer months in seclusion. In the winter months I would practice with my golf mind that I learned to activate from George Knudson in the late seventies.

I would visualize the positions I wanted to achieve during the swing process that combined well with muscle memory I secured from rigorous practice with Moe. My movements were developed similar to the way Moe moved. When I could not hit balls, the visualization still allowed me to practice as if I were hitting golf balls.

There has been a misconception relayed to the public to convince golfers that Moe Norman swung the golf club differently than the conventional golf swing. These hybrid swing methods that gathered some exposure separated his action from his traditional golf swing. As a result golfers were lead in the wrong direction from the true Moe Norman golf swing. Moe had a golf swing that was truly traditional and the evidence from the sixties and seventies proves this. The observations of Moe's golf swing by these method chasers that got it wrong were twenty to thirty years late and missed out on his traditional perfected golf swing. I have brought it back to the public. The true way Moe Norman swung the golf club could be compared to Byron Nelson, Ben Hogan, and Ken Venturi.

Moe had a different style of set up from the conventional address position, though his manufactured swing had many similarities in comparison to the legendary ball strikers. Lee Trevino whom I consider a legendary ball striker was winning on the tour during the seventies. Trevino on the down swing and through the ball had noticeable similarities.

The golf swing, to Moe, is one that must be delivered — all in one package — on time and without artificial moves. Artificial moves would only destroy the direction of the clubface when making contact with the ball.

A solid impact position is the result of things you did in your swing prior to it, to make it happen. Moe stressed the importance of how to create the necessary lag to retain the angle at pre-impact for solid contact.

Moe appeared different to the general public with a social perspective from experiences that he faced as a poor man trying to make it at a rich man's game. Moe was labeled an outcast that suffered internally from a social disorder. Moe would put up walls where loneliness became his way of life. His escape was security with a few close friends in his inner circle he trusted. Moe was shy and socially unable to be his funny outgoing self without finding trouble. It was loneliness that put Moe's concentration in the direction of hitting golf balls to become an incredible ball striker which became his comfort to ease the loneliness particularly in the early years. Moe knew his own moves better than anyone else and could explain his swing clearly and precisely from ball beating.

I could never understand the golf professionals who tried to promote that Moe did not know how to explain what he does. How absurd and foolish, these egotistical fools would never know where to start. Moe did not have the elaborate teacher's lingo and his presentation may have lacked the fluent vocabulary, though he knew the golf swing and explained it with his own vocabulary. During the years I spent with Moe, his terminology became broader from Paul Bertholy's book that provided an intellectual confidence with aspirations to speak more fluently in public.

To set the record straight, Moe Norman was not autistic. No Rain Man here!

From my own lips, "I strongly believe that Moe could have never taught me or explained in such great detail to swing the golf club in his own likeness if he experienced autism."

Moe's genius should have been appreciated rather than labeled with a condition for a few that saw an opportunity to make a movie. I would support a movie of the greatest ball striker in the world but never label my friend with autism when he is not. This was a ridiculous ploy only to minimize Moe as a uniquely talented individual that just did things different. His unique style brought attention to him that allowed people to selfishly start false rumors rather than give the entitled recognition to a golfer dedicated for great achievement.

Moe was usually given a hard time by PGA tour officials where his great talent was not enough to excuse him from the ill treatment he received.

Some was his fault, and some was directed personally at him from his lack of fashion particularly in the early years. Moe was his own man with no intention of going down to the low level of kissing someone's ass. Moe missed the big tour and in his later years wished that circumstances could have brought acceptance rather than rejection. Acceptance of Moe was displayed from Ken Venturi and Sam Snead who appreciated Moe's ability to strike the golf ball so pure at impact. Snead gave Moe a lesson when a young amateur.

Venturi called him "Pipeline Moe" out of respect as the one most likely to roll it down the sprinkler system. The players and officials that did not welcome him in Canada and the United States forced Moe to suck up the jealousy from the upper crust. If Moe could have hung in longer on the PGA tour, in time he would have belonged and won numerous tour events including a US Open.

After leaving the tour with a third place finish at New Orleans, he demonstrated an awesome performance with the best players in the world. Moe decided to concentrate on ball striking and setting course records. When Moe spoke to me on this subject he felt a smaller guy could become the best ball striker of all time. Moe said, "I feel I have now done that and become a pretty good player also." Moe traveled the tournament circuit in Canada and helped many tour players improve who were struggling to make tournament cuts on various tours. Moe never had to market himself as a teacher where the professionals new of his talent and knowledge. Moe just walked on the range at the tournament site and top tour stars would abandon their practice session for a closer view with hopes of learning something new. One of Moe's favorite tournament sites was the Canadian Open when the US PGA tour players arrived for their practice rounds.

Moe was finally recognized by the Royal Canadian Golf Association during 1995 Inducted into the Canadian Golf Hall Of Fame.

Unfortunately for Moe and the public it was twenty years too late and the real appreciation was lost by Moe.

There is no reason to go over the details when it was pure jealousy and animosity from the RCGA held over the years against Moe without valid reasons. Moe was very appreciative to the fans for their persistence to induct him into his rightful place. I sometimes wonder where we get these individuals that have little logic and closed minds that operate our associations. It is my hope that the RCGA and Golfers learn from the past and make decisions on performance going forward.

In 2004, nine years after his induction into the Hall of Fame he passed away with heart problems. There are many people that miss him in the golfing world, which included both friends and fans. Moe had a great career in Canadian golf and became known for his ball striking worldwide. I regret not being able to make it to his funeral. I miss him and think of him all the time especially when I put the golf swing he taught me into action. I hope this book will be a great tribute to his legacy that I promised to write when I last spoke to Moe.

It has been many years since I was a skinny kid walking the fairways with insight into the world of Moe that shaped me with his magic moves. The more I practiced the better understanding I developed towards purity of technique. The other valuable lesson I learned was to never give up. This is something that stayed inside me for many years. It was the important connection between golf and life in the attempt of reaching your full potential. Truth was our bond. Our friendship inspired us to keep the golf dream alive that Moe Norman made possible.

I graduated with a Bachelors of Arts Degree from University of Prince Edward Island in May 1993. When Moe visited me in Charlottetown he hoped I would use my new University education to write a golf book. "Hopefully smart enough."

Greg at impact 2010, Halifax, NS. Canada

Moe at impact 1964, Ormond Beach, Florida

Chapter 7 –
Swing Photos of Moe Norman 1964

*set-up with high hands and wide stance
stretch away from ball on backswing*

*rotation of hips and shoulders
left foot raises up as right hip goes up*

relaxed left arm at top of swing
in the batter's box totally centered

left palm pushes downward to right heel
left knee leads with great separation

elbows lead shaft that continues way out
right knee works in behind left knee

left shoulder up with bowed left wrist
club face square low and long

eye's focus is over right knee
right ear lays down on right shoulder

shoulders rotate on plane
bowed left wrist continues up the line

natural clearance of left side not forced
complete weight transfer to left leg

high finish with great balance
starting to recess with target focus

Moe displays a full extension with an awesome finish to the sky.
This is truly the best Moe Norman swung the golf club.

left arm and shaft one straight line
right hip goes up and turns with coil

left comes up with full body coil
navel going to ball

right hand hits on its own accord
release beyond ball

Swing Photos of Moe's Student Greg Lavern

stretching back
shoulders and hips rotate

left palm down to right heel
beyond impact square face

playing into my legs
right instep just starting to rise

finish with great balance
extend over the target

Iron Swing Sequence Greg Lavern

left palm down to right heel
shaft and left arm straight line

Working up the line
finish to the sky

Greg View from the Back

stretch and reach back
hips and shoulders rotate
elbows lead

left knee drives forward
right instep stays down
weight transfer R to L

high finish in balance

Moe Norman View from the Back

stretching on the takeaway
hips and shoulders coiled
vertical drop elbows lead

left knee works down the line
eyes focus over right knee
working the line with left wrist

hip clearance never forced
finish in balance
target oriented

Wide stance, high hands and club head behind ball.

Chapter 8 –
The Moe Norman Grip

There has been some controversy on the Moe Norman grip where pure principals must be put in their proper perspective. It is important to realize that Moe used a variation of the actual Vardon grip that Ben Hogan invented for his own personal use. This was his original grip Moe used when winning many tournaments and setting course records. Grip the golf club in Moe and Hogan fashion to abolish any foolishness that was promoted about Moe using a baseball grip when playing tournament golf. The baseball grip was part and parcel of a phony method that Moe was directed to perform during Natural Golf clinics. Moe used the Overlap grip for many years with great success and changed for showmanship only when requested under his Natural Golf contract.

In this section I will explain how the man with the best pair of hands in golf held on to his golf club. It is important to understand the sole purpose of gripping the golf club was to hold on. The original grip Moe used for many years produced much more solid contact. You want to create unity of the left and right hand that will mold the hands together as one unit. Moe always disagreed with the saying, "Grip the golf grip like a bird." Moe wanted firmness to grasp the golf club with authority that insured passive hands with the desire to feel the club head was not flimsy. The firmness in the palms and fingers should still maintain soft wrists flexible without tension that Moe and I felt.

The grip you select is your own preference whether the Baseball, Inter-lock, Overlap, or the Ben Hogan and Moe Norman selection with the slight variation from the original Vardon grip. There have been many great players that utilized other grip styles with no set way to grip the golf club based on their personal preference. My concentration is how Moe Norman actually gripped the club. Your selection of grip style must perform the important duty to hold on to the golf club in wet or humid weather.

Moe Norman used the overlapped grip to win all his tournaments.

The Left Hand:

Moe was left handed and swung the golf club right handed the same way Ben Hogan did, that put the dominate strength in their lead arm and hand. Moe utilized his left hand strength where he squeezed his last three fingers with firmness in an attempt to draw blood. This was a feeling Moe had when he grabbed the golf club in his left hand even if blood was not actually drawn.

The grip would lay diagonally across the palm just above his callus line and underneath the heel pad. He formed a trigger finger as Hogan did to balance the golf grip that allowed the forefinger knuckle to stick out. The left was turned slightly clockwise to view at least three knuckles that is considered a strong left hand grip. Moe felt he was making a fist with the left thumb slightly over to the right side of the grip with a high oval wrist bone as he addressed the ball.

It should be understood that even though the golf club was in the palm of the left hand it was his squeezed fingers that created a combination of palm and fingers. Moe would squeeze a tennis ball to increase his left hand strength for firmness in his last three fingers.

Greg Lavern demonstrates the left hand grip with high oval wrist.

The Right Hand:

Moe's right hand was above the callus line, different from Hogan's whose was below, which put the golf club more in the fingers. Moe's right hand grip was initially in his fingers though the grip thickness with five to six layers of tape pushed the golf grip higher into the palm of the right hand. The little finger of the right hand would lie across and around the knuckle of the left hand.

This was the difference or variation between the actual grip Ben Hogan and Moe Norman preferred rather than the simplified Vardon grip. The across and wrap around effect of the right baby finger to the left hand forefinger secures a firmer grip and higher right hand that would increase the unity of the right and left hand. The right hand grip pressure was from the two middle fingers of the right hand while the right thumb laid slightly to the left of the grip. Moe applied firm, adequate grip pressure with the right hand even though the right hand was only along for the ride.

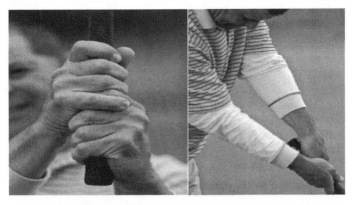

Front View of Overlap Grip Right and Left Hand Unity

Moe's Grip:

When Moe had both hands on the golf club he would lift up from the back of the grip to raise his wrists extremely high. Comparatively, the low hands in the traditional grip looked unorthodox to him. Moe's left hand was strong in appearance though the grip remained in the palm with secured pressure from his last three fingers. Moe use to say, "I have the perfect grip." The golf club was held the same way regardless if he wanted to fade or draw the ball and would make a stance adjustment to work the golf ball at will. To hold the golf club the same way is the best way without change or variation that will eventually become second nature. Moe would grip approximately one and a half to two inches down the grip for control from driver through wedge.

This gripped-down feature produced more solid contact and straightness for Moe that was useful when in between clubs or when a knock down shot was required. By not gripping the golf club towards the end of the grip produced a loss of distance. Gripping down forced him to hit one more club than normal since he preferred control over distance. That was paramount in Moe's mind.

Moe's grip forced the hands to mold together, that encouraged the back of the left hand to ride the line while the silent right hand would go directly at the flag stick on the follow through. The ball goes where the hands go so that never allowed the hands to fight once his natural relay of power from unified hands was directed to the club head. I highly recommend this style of grip Moe used during his early golf career as your starting point to perform the rest of the movements.

Chapter 9 –
Moe Norman Set-up

Pre-Shot Routine

Moe started his pre-shot routine twenty yards before his golf ball to size up the situation for a clear understanding of his target or the type of shot required. There was no fooling around with Moe taking just seconds to place the club head behind the ball. With one waggle the ball was launched. It would start when he drew his golf club out of the bag with confidence knowing that was the proper shot with no second thoughts or indecision. Moe could see the results of his shot in his own mind through visualization while walking up to his shot. The visualization continued while over the ball until he elected to pull the trigger and fire at his target.

Moe would pick out a cloud in the sky or a tree top from a scenic background lined up with his intended target.

Moe approached the golf ball from the side and not the traditional way of approaching from behind the shot. In Moe's eyes this was a waste of time since he was ready from preparation of going through a pre-shot routine before he approached his golf ball. The head of the golf club was placed well behind the ball as his starting point with both hands on the golf grip. There was none of this left hand first followed by the right hand into position. The approach, with two hands on the golf club, demonstrated confidence with one waggle to feel the club head. The one waggle approach helped to initiate a smooth flowing action on his back swing without hesitation.

Moe would say, "Bad thoughts cause bad shots." Moe displayed a pre-shot routine that had the same consistency to eliminate any negative thoughts. He would keep moving without hesitation from start to completion of his golf swing. Moe developed a pre-shot routine that flowed directly into a solid set-up which is paramount for good ball striking. If you set-up properly like Moe it will increase your chances to hit more solid golf shots since you have started properly out of the gate.

Moe would place the driver head fourteen inches behind the ball with his eyes close to seven inches behind the ball. It became an instant reaction for his arms to extend fully with high hands as his legs spread extremely wide. Moe's stance was wider than shoulder width with weight on his heels and evenly distributed inside the insteps. His right foot remained at right angles to secure the weight transferred inside the right leg on the back swing. The left foot was toed out forty- five degrees for a solid weight transfer laterally. During his early amateur years he stood pigeon toed that would ensure an incredibly straight shot but would lose distance. In later years Moe elected to point his left foot out that provided more power and clearance of the left side.

With straight rigid legs and his rear end sticking out, his stance encouraged bending from the hip joints to maintain his spine angle in perfect proportion during the set-up. The top of the left shoulder was pointed high at his intended target with one straight line from the top of the shoulder to the club head.

The shaft is connected to become an extension of his left arm. Moe's right arm stayed relaxed or in the crooked position underneath the left arm. Moe wanted a club to fit through his arms to ensure the right arm was lower than the left. This was different from the majority of golfers that choose to set the right arm equal or higher on their way to disaster with their shoulders going over top of the legs far too soon.

Moe lifted underneath the grip to create high hands that encouraged soft wrists, tension free. His left wrist was high and oval the same as the right wrist though more relaxed from the crooked right arm. The left hand V went toward his chest rather than the right shoulder from the golf club fourteen inches behind the ball much different than the normal golfer. Moe's right hand V in the grip would point directly to his right shoulder. The face of his driver was square to the target or just a fraction to the right, since Moe would line up toward the heel of the driver where I preferred the face centered to the ball. Iron shots were slightly different with the club face lined up in conjunction with the leading edge that ensured a perfectly square blade to the target.

Moe's ball position with the driver was on the inside thigh of the left leg while his ball position was centered for normal iron shots. If the shot required a lower trajectory Moe would position the golf ball more toward the right foot. When Moe needed a higher flight he would move the ball a couple of inches forward. To fade it required forward movement of the right foot or backward to draw the ball. Moe adjusted his stance to work the golf ball at will while knowing the club path and swing plane would change slightly to work the ball in various directions when required. Moe never turned his golf grip to hit a fade or hook as this was inconsistent for tournament play and utilized stance adjustment.

Moe Norman set-up 1964

Here is Moe with focus on the club head twelve to fourteen inches behind the golf ball, Moe Norman style. The V of the right hand points to the right shoulder while the left hand V points to his chest. One straight line of left arm and shaft supported with a wide stance, forming a tripod.

Moe's desired set-up looked unorthodox compared to other golfers that choose to stand narrow with no foundation that can be totally unstable in bad weather. Moe had a strong foundation with his wide stance and high hand position that braced him solid in the wind. The wider stance on the set up will promote great leg action and eliminate the shoulders from going over the top of the legs too soon.

When taking aim at a target, Moe would align the top of the left shoulder to a cloud or tree top with the driver and with his irons he would aim over top of the flag stick. Moe formed a K position when ready to start his swing. Moe kept the club head active to keep his flow not to freeze at address. Moe would set the club fourteen inches behind the ball after one waggle of the club head that returned to his original starting position, ready to put his back swing into motion.

Greg Lavern Back View

Front View of Moe's Setup 1963

Back View of Moe's Setup 1963

Chapter 10 –
The Moe Norman Back Swing

Moe squeezes the last three fingers with left wrist rotation that enables the left arm to go across his chest. With a high oval left wrist starting position, the hands do not drop as the club extends back. The feeling is to STRETCH BACK as the wrists cock naturally upward while the shoulders and hips continue rotation from the starting position. Stretching away from the ball really creates enormous width in Moe's back swing with a head start of having the club head fourteen inches behind the ball. There are two other positives existing here because the club head can't be taken outside and the club head can't be taken back any lower on the take away from being fourteen inches into it at address.

Moe allows his right hip to go up and then clears naturally with the weight staying inside the right leg or thigh. The weight actually goes to the right heel for extra clearance of the right side while the right leg stays firm to insure the weight shift on the backswing stays inside the right instep. Moe starts with his weight evenly distributed between the insteps. His left foot comes off the ground rolling on the front instep from his wide stance and extreme turning of the hips and shoulders. The left knee goes outward and turns toward the ball to allow the weight transfer loading to the right heel. This happens easily since Moe's center or chest turns completely facing outward over the right foot. Near the top of his back swing, his right arm aids the balance of the club head and the hands get higher. Moe's eyes focus on the club head and stay there while the left shoulder goes under and rubs his chin.

His left wrist is flat at the top of the back swing with the right palm under the shaft. The right elbow points down with a slight bend in the left arm that allows elastic flexibility for his left arm lever to continue. The club shaft is parallel at the top of the swing with his irons and slightly over parallel when swinging his driver where the club face faces the sky. Moe would always say, "The back swing does not hit the ball. It flows to set everything up."

Moe's back swing has great tempo that encourages smooth centrifugal force.

Moe Norman's 1964 backswing with total rotation of hips and shoulders

Greg Lavern's backswing 2012

Moe Norman stretches away and allows his elbow to fold and point to the ground.

Chapter 11 –
The Downswing

The left foot elevates and gracefully the left heel is placed back on the ground with a flexed left knee to move forward down the target line. This will cause the right instep to roll down on the ground with a pushing action from the right instep for great separation and proper use of the legs laterally. Moe puts himself into an outstanding sitting position where the weight remains on his heels.

When the transition takes place as a component of the proper sequence of motion, this makes the vertical drop an automatic action. His left palm and arm pushes downward at the right heel while the club head is still behind him.

Moe's left side leads the way to utilize his left deltoid muscle below the shoulder or full connection of the left arm and shaft. As the left arm pulls forward both elbows lead the arms and hands to retain the right side from prematurely hitting too soon. From the transition or vertical drop there is the feeling of the lower half starting before completion of the backswing. Some have called it "the crossroads of golf". Moe felt his hands were way back and in position to extend the shaft way out beyond the impact zone when starting down.

The left arm lever continues with left side dominance while the butt of the grip points toward the back of the golf ball. Moe stays behind the golf ball in the batter's box centered to eliminate the upper body from sliding forward with lower body driving forward. This insures the right palm skyward in the karate chop position like holding a tray of drinks level.

There is a bow in his right side at pre-impact while the left arm leader is higher than the retained right arm and hand on a forty five degree angle. Moe leads with the heel of the club head to eliminate a lively toe. The clubface squares up on its own accord from the outstanding pre-impact position that Moe puts himself into. Moe's weight is all on his left foot while he retains the shaft angle at pre-impact before he reaches impact.

Moe achieves his impact position with a straight line from the top of left shoulder to a square club face, in comparison to the position he started, with the exception of maintaining his left knee flexed and lateral motion coming into impact. When the shaft leads beyond the golf ball that pulls the left arm and hand away from the left side. And this keeps the club face square for a long period of time through impact. Both arms start to level out with the right slightly lower than the left from the initial crooked right arm lower than the left and that is maintained at impact.

As Moe leads with the shaft his feeling is four feet in front of him and the same impact position is achieved without artificial methods through impact. When the shaft extends, the right hand is in position to provide a little more power. The right hand hits while the shaft is extended and that causes "penetration" or shaft flex through the hitting area. Moe never thinks of impact as the ball just gets in the way of the club face from his previous movements. When you hit through the ball like Moe the club face always catches up to a square position.

Moe created a late hit by leading with the heel of the club and put his right hand in a wonderful position to hit with unforced power. There was a low spot in Moe's swing path caused from the shaft leading while the left arm and hand moved away from the left side that enabled him to continue up the line.

From the connection of the left arm, hand and shaft extending way out forms the horizontal tug. This continued action happens once the left hand rides the line for a long period of time before his right side releases with the right hand and arm in-line with the flag stick.

Once his right shoulder starts to work under his chin on the through swing the right back muscle adds power as the natural rotation of the shoulders work back on the same swing plane. When the extended horizontal tug can't go any further laterally then the lower body rotation starts and is followed by the shoulder rotation that clears the left side on its own accord.

Greg vertical drop 2012
Greg vertical drop 2009
Greg black belt since 2002

You could place a tray on my right hand. The golf swing and martial arts have similarities in their execution, particularly on the downswing.

Lead with the legs and lag the hands riding the line and leading with the butt.

Moe's downswing secures a bowed left wrist through impact and beyond that never breaks down. His downswing is left side dominant with the right side relaxed and retained. When the proper sequence of motion flows maximum speed at impact is achieved: the moment of truth.

Chapter 12 –
Moe's Finish

Moe would ride the line upward and swung within the golf course knowing the ball goes where his hands go. As the rotation of the shoulders work themselves back on plane, the right foot comes off the ground to balance on his right toe with his chest facing the target. His left side forms one straight line with his entire weight on a flat left foot in perfect balance. Moe's swing balances him which is the natural result from his ability to play into his legs. This starts from the transition point where the legs support a fantastic sitting position before striking the golf ball with weight on his heels.

In order to maintain good balance it is important to hold the finish. Moe would swing at eighty percent for solid contact that produces straightness and distance. Moe always had twenty yards in reserve when it was necessary to let out the shaft.

Moe's tempo stayed within himself from start to finish. Tempo can be faster or slower as long as it remains the same. The longer Moe stayed over the ball with good tempo the more this contributed to staying centered which is a requirement for great balance.

He stabilized with balance to the finish. Moe would say, "I never let the golf ball control me." Moe had perfect balance throughout his entire golf swing. Once Moe completed his normal finish he continued to point the club head to the sky with a recess of arms to his target. During the sixties his arm recesses were brought down in front of him in a lower position that relaxed the arms.

When I knew Moe in the seventies, his arm recess pointed to the sky from a more target-oriented mind that triggered his reaction to the sky.

Moe focused with great control and balance on the flight of the golf ball. Moe would play target golf while watching the flight that helped secure his balance and unique finish.

Moe high finish before extension to the sky

Greg shows great balance

Greg relaxed in balance while he finishes over the tree tops

Moe extends his club over the tree tops to the clouds.

Chapter 13 –
The Importance of the Vertical Drop

The vertical drop known to many as the transition or the crossroads of golf is the slot position that allows the arms and hands to swing squarely into impact with total left side control. Moe's right side and hand was retained. That encouraged a late release where his shoulder rotation continued back on plane after impact.

The first secret Moe explained to me was how the left palm goes to the right heel while the entire left forearm is pushing downward. This is the vertical drop and if done with this movement the weight shift will happen automatically. Once you have this movement down you will be positioning the club with similarities of the great ball strikers. The club face will lag behind while the left side continues lateral down the line since the legs are forced to move forward from the vertical drop.

The advanced player that has fairly good leg action will experience the vertical drop from movement that happens before the transition takes place. I will give you something Moe drove into me as his young student: When starting the downswing, feel you are pushing off the right instep with the energy going to the top of the left shoulder while there is a pulling from inside the left knee that leads the swing. If this is done properly the vertical drop will happen as a result of proper use of the legs and left shoulder generating upwards. Moe would say, "What goes up must come down." When the left shoulder goes up and the left knee leads there is great separation of the left and right knee. This creates the vertical drop where the hands and arms have dropped behind you.

Hogan used to try and put his hands in his back pocket for extra lead and lag. The club lags behind as the top of the left shoulder generates skyward. This allows the right elbow to lead the hands that becomes automatic without the need to drive the right elbow inward artificially.

The vertical drop was a term introduced by Paul Bertholy. Moe used to describe his transition coordinated with other Bertholy terms "buckle, sit, slide and bump" as Moe returned to impact with his left wrist bowed through the golf ball. Moe started with the weight on his heels and pushed off his right in-step with the energy generating to his left shoulder that allowed him to sit down through impact. The buckled left knee continued with a forward pulling action from inside the left thigh. Moe's leg action and elevation of the left shoulder coordinated together allow the vertical drop to happen on its own accord.

While Moe and I were hitting balls together, I had the butt end of the club going down toward the ground on my transition. Moe came over and pushed down on my left arm before I reached the top of my swing. He gave me the feeling of how the bottom starts before the club reaches completion of the back swing. In essence the legs have already started while the golf club is still going back.

The left palm and arm pushed downward in an attempt to cover the right heel as the club shaft dropped behind from the transfer of weight from right to left. His knees separated with the left knee driving forward as the club head was dropping behind creating tremendous lag of the shaft and club head.

Once the left palm pushed downward, the right elbow would move tight to the right side. The butt of the grip pointed down the fairway where the heel would lead to eliminate early activity from the toe of the club head.

Moe explained and demonstrated his transition while he performed it. I hope this has cleared up many misconceptions on Moe's true vertical drop. I experienced it firsthand one summer day in 1982 at Golf Haven G.C.

This was a productive and memorable day as Moe incorporated the vertical drop into my golf swing the proper way, his way. This is how the straightest ball striker in the world approached his transition or, in Bertholy terminology, the vertical drop.

Greg Lavern's vertical drop from behind

Moe Norman shows his vertical drop from front and back

Chapter 14 –
Moe's Horizontal Tug

Moe stayed behind the golf ball for a long time while he struck it through impact. He would describe this to me when using the terminology, "staying in the batter's box." Moe, like many of the great ball strikers got the club head back on the ground early to hit the ball first. This positioned the club face to stay low and long beyond the ball. The result was divots like bacon strips beyond or in front of the ball. It should be noted the bottom of the arc is when the club bottoms out before the golf ball. The bottom of the arc for Moe, Hogan and many great ball strikers was different than instruction today where instructors want the club head to bottom out at the ball. This is one of the reasons modern day tour players take big hamburgers for divots. Moe and Hogan preferred long thin bacon strips rather than the club head on the ball for a mere instant.

Moe hit through the ball with his left arm and hand down the line with separation of the left arm and hand from the left side. The club face remained square as the left arm and bowed left wrist extended down his target line.

When fully extended the back of the left wrist would ride the line to the sky. This was another Bertholy term Moe used to describe his forward and outward extension called the Horizontal Tug. This takes place when the left arm and hand are tugging forward down the line after impact. The Horizontal was certainly not the pulling or tugging from inside the left thigh when the left knee moved laterally to the target as many searching for rainbows have claimed.

From my personal instruction with Moe Norman and two visits to Paul Bertholy I provide the Horizontal Tug terminology with my own description.

"THE HORIZONTAL TUG INVOLVES CONTINUATION OF A STRAIGHT LEFT ARM AND HAND WHILE FOCUSING ON THE SHAFT THREE OR FOUR FEET IN FRONT OF THE IMPACT WITH THE BALL. THE ULTIMATE PENDULUM POSITION IS WHERE THE SHAFT AND CLUB HEAD HANG VERTICALLY PAST IMPACT."

It should be understood the Horizontal Tug would be the key for Moe to eliminate the left side of the golf course. There was minimum rotation in Moe's left arm extension that happened naturally from his shoulder rotation and late release.

Moe's left arm extended for the longest time and continued from his superb left arm radius created from his back swing. With a continued bowed wrist, both arms extended down the line and he felt he was extending from his under arm sockets. The left arm is a rifle barrel while the right hand shakes the flag stick.

It should be noted that Paul Bertholy had a much shorter horizontal tug than Moe or me, where he allowed his left hand to turn over early with the left palm facing the sky to promote a draw. Moe completed the horizontal tug with his left wrist skyward and the left palm pointing to the ground. This action kept the clubface square not only through impact but through the upward swing; that is a major requirement to achieve the true pendulum action for straightness and accuracy.

Moe was very secretive about how he reached pendulum which occurs when the shaft is hanging vertically out front. This is how Moe got his incredible ball flight. Moe explained and connected his final secret that I will provide in the next chapter. When the final secret is executed with pendulum, real purity and straightness will be achieved.

The horizontal tug will bring you to pendulum as our mind senses the shaft is hanging vertically in front of you with both hands on the golf club. Moe and I think three to four feet in front of us.

Greg demonstrates a great extension with a strong left arm and hand.

Greg from a different angle

Chapter 15 –
Moe Norman's Final Secrets to Greg Lavern

It has been amazing that golf instruction teachers have continued to explore the reasons behind Moe Norman's ability to hit the golf ball so pure with character.

Unfortunately, these enthusiastic promoters of Moe's golf swing made their own observations with lots of hogwash to fool the public. It is understandable that these opportunists would not know his true golf swing since Moe told them nothing of importance. I have listened. None have the knowledge I have kept safe for years from my long personal practice and playing relationship with my buddy Moe. I can honestly say the material in this book is the real deal of how Moe approached his golf swing. I felt it important to reveal my true important knowledge to eliminate any further guessing regarding Moe Norman's golf swing.

Moe had incredible ball flight with character and with a much different trajectory than other professional golfers. The golf ball would travel straight up to the clouds with minimum or no side spin that would drop straight down from the sky. There were many white golf balls against a blue sky that landed softly like butterflies. Moe would hit his driver on a tight driving hole straight as an arrow within a ten foot square in the middle of the fairway. If he attacked a tight pin placement the golf ball would stop on hard green surfaces. Moe would say, "Flight tells all."

From my close relationship, I was the one Moe had chosen to keep his important secrets safe and was free to write a book after his death.

Moe assured Lawson and me that no one else knows. Moe would never lie to either of us since our relationship was built on honesty and trust or Moe would not want anything to do with you. Moe gave me the opportunity to learn personally from him with private teachings. I hope to do him justice so his legacy and my deliverance of his golf swing will help golfers become better ball strikers.

Besides the basic things Moe told me while shaping my swing in his own likeness, there were three special secrets he provided to myself and assured me that no one else knows. The first one was how Moe performed the vertical drop. The second was related to his downswing and the third was what Hogan never told the public which Moe incorporated long ago.

It was during one of our practice sessions in the late seventies at Golf Haven G.C. when Moe started to give me a speech. Moe said, "There are millions of people out there who want to figure out what I do. They all want what I have. Now old buddy you will know what I do, the only one. I wanted you to know for what I think of you and how close you move like me. You will get it in your swing and be able to teach greatness."

Moe would get quite emotional from time to time then give me a big bear hug. I would never show pain or any sign of being wimpy. I only showed appreciation and would be strong and looked Moe straight in the eyes. He knew he was my best friend and teacher.

Moe use to say, "We are two hard working guys pal. I only ask, don't tell anyone until I am six feet under." I kept my promise and never told anyone for all these years except basic things which was ok with Moe.

It is my opinion that Moe really wanted to be around me since I would do him no harm and we both were extremely dedicated toward learning as much as possible about hitting the golf ball pure. Why me? I was capable of easily adapting to his principles and was learning identical moves. Moe was not interested in telling someone that swung high through the ball and spun like a top. Moe had his own reasons that never changed despite the false claims others have made. I never expected anything from Moe or asked him for anything which he greatly appreciated. He gave me his special knowledge as his gift to me. This was Moe's way of saying "thank you" for our long golfing relationship and friendship.

When playing golf or on the practice tee, we were by ourselves and talked about many things besides the golf swing. Moe would tell me his inner most feelings and sensed I was going through the same things with people in authority that he experienced during his golf career. Moe encouraged me to become my own man.

Moe was no ass kisser and said what he felt. Moe said, "If I knew what I know now things would have been much easier. Still hit balls but in a smart way."

I asked, "How Moe?"

Then Moe tapped me a couple of times on the noodle, "The mind working together with the golf swing is a powerful weapon with less effort."

Before the final secrets are revealed I would like to make a suggestion. If your intention is to incorporate these secrets into your golf swing it would be advisable to follow up with myself. I plan to have my own website to teach the golf swing Moe taught me for many years. I am the true authority and expert when it comes to the actual way Moe Norman swung the golf club. If I was to recommend anyone other than myself to teach Moe's swing it would be Lawson Mitchell or my student Tim Lynch. There will be self proclaimed professionals or instructors that will take your money and attempt to teach the knowledge from this book with as much understanding as you. For success and results it would be advisable to seek out the true living source.

Flight tells how you performed the moves in the golf swing that separates the great ball strikers from the pack. Moe would say, "Pendulum was the closest thing to a perfect swing." We think of pendulum in the putting stroke when the putter swings back and forth. This is comparable in the full swing where the club face stays square as long as physically possible for absolute straightness. When Moe spoke about pendulum it was beyond impact and continued to complete the swing. The incredible flight Moe achieved was a result of the club face long and low beyond impact; his strong automatic left arm dominance known as the horizontal tug lead to his ultimate pendulum position. When Moe and I practiced we would hit one arm wedges with the left arm only. Hitting these shots demanded the left arm would extend fully after striking the golf ball with the shaft.

The shaft and club head was positioned vertically from the continuation of the horizontal tug's left arm extension. During an actual golf shot with two hands on the golf club, the perfect pendulum position was achieved as the right shoulder works under the chin that squares the right hand up from the retained tray position at post impact. You will always hit through the ball from the shaft extension not just to impact where a majority of amateurs and professionals release the golf club prematurely. The release should be well in front of you when the horizontal tug sets up. When executed properly, the heel of the golf club will be leading with no activity in the toe. Moe would hit with the shaft as the top of the left shoulder generated skyward. The butt of the grip is actually pulled over the left shoulder which strikes the golf ball with the shaft. This is followed by an automatic impact position as the square face follows its consistent path.

It is important to understand that through the proper sequence of motion the vertical drop or transition happens naturally with the left palm going to the right heel as the left arm pushes downward.

Moe's golf swing was a full pendulum motion where the vertical drop and horizontal tug allowed the hands to follow a pendulum path. Moe knew the ball would go where his hands went. He swung within the golf course and the hands never went out of bounds. It should be noted that the right arm is lower than the left, rubbing the chest with the right elbow through impact. Both Moe Norman and Ben Hogan developed their right hand to retain and never hit too soon.

Hogan's toe of the club was more active than Moe's into impact with a desire to square the face early from the fast clearance of Hogan's hips. Moe would work down the line laterally much longer, producing a much squarer club face through impact and beyond. Moe hit it straight, which was no accident, where as Hogan had to work the ball. The golfer that can maintain a squarer club face for a longer period of time will hit it straighter. This is why Moe released the club in a different way much later than other golfers.

Moe's own words to me. "Lead with the heel into a pendulum position that will allow the horizontal tug to continue with the back of my left wrist lifting upward to the finish as the right hand naturally shakes hands with the flag stick. This eliminates any twisting or turning in my swing. I swing through the golf course, never out of bounds." I want to feel the club head and shaft hanging way out in front of me way past impact, straight up and down in pendulum. I think four feet in front of me."

Secret One: **The left palm goes to the right heel on transition known as the vertical drop**. This is a result of how the downswing is started that creates the transition of dropping with weight transfer. This positioning is referred to as the "master move" by Moe Norman and Ben Hogan. When the transition takes place there is more cocking on the way down where both Moe and Hogan attempted to put their hands in their back pocket. The Left palm and arm pushes toward the right heel.

Secret Two: **Think way back and way out**. The way back is the vertical drop where the cocking of the wrists is working behind Moe. This is done actually from the deltoid muscle behind the left shoulder that will create more width on the vertical drop. The way out is the shaft hitting the golf ball and the feeling of continuation four feet in front of that. This can also be executed with the grip pulling over the left shoulder to simplify left arm extension or the horizontal tug that will be achieved from the execution of the way out. Moe wanted the shaft to hang vertically way out in front of him at pendulum. The way out of the shaft naturally moves the left arm outward away from the left side after impact with a naturally bowed left wrist that works down the line and up the line.

You will never have to worry what is happening at impact or have to manipulate your impact position since the ball is just getting in the way of a club head hitting through the golf ball.

Secret Three: This is the most important secret of the three as this is what Moe did but also the secret Hogan never told the public and saved for himself. There were only three people that actually knew it. Moe, Hogan from their personal conversations and the secret passed on to me. Moe had me doing the same move as Hogan and himself when I was a young professional. The secret is when Moe and Hogan **started their downswing with the navel or stomach going directly outward to the ball**. Amazing things happen from this. The vertical drop is a natural reaction from the navel moving forward toward the ball with the weight on the heels in an outstanding sitting position.

When the stomach or navel moves forward toward the ball, this allows the hands and arms to work properly with the elbows leading into post impact. This was how Moe played into his legs, creating a bow of the right side into impact with a flexed or buckled left knee and his right instep pushing into the ground with a forward force going one way while a resisting force going the other way.

This generates in one direction while retaining in the other. This centered Moe in the batter's box and allowed his golf swing to balance him. Moe would say, "My golf swing balances me."

Moe would casually tell people that Hogan and he had the master move. Many people thought the vertical drop alone was the master move. Actually there were a few moves that involved the concept of "way back" and "way out" that required the proper sequence of motion. The stomach to the ball is the key to start the downswing, and the vertical drop is a result that follows in the sequence. As Hogan once said, "It is right there if you know what to look for". Little did the public know that both Moe and Hogan had the same secret. Now you know Moe Norman's three final secrets he provided to me that included the Hogan secret that I know is authentic and true. Moe Norman would have no reason to lie as perfect as he hit the golf ball all his life. I can now say I have delivered the most important keys to the golf swing as promised.

Moe's Final Secrets

Navel to ball as Moe strives to put his hands in his back pocket.

Vertical drop where the left palm and arm pushes down naturally to the right heel.

Moe will continue with the shaft **"WAY OUT"** while in his mind he sees four feet in front of him. The result, an automatic pure impact position where the shaft hits the golf ball.

Chapter 16 –
Bunker Play and Short Shots

Moe would set up for a bunker shot with the club face square rather than opening the blade to get loft as most tour players would prefer. For a normal bunker shot the weight distribution stays inside his insteps. Moe utilized the sole or bottom of his Sandy Andy to bounce into the sand. The larger sole established more bounce, so there is limited digging to allow the leading edge to cut level through the sand. The majority of weight on his left foot would elevate the club upright on the back swing. His knees freely moved forward with the feeling of spanking the sand with the sole of the club head.

When Moe entered the bunker he worked both feet into the sand for better footage with a feel for sand texture that could be fine or heavy. Observation of the sand texture provided insight as to how the ball would react on the green and determine the best area to land his shot. Normally he would hit a couple of inches behind the ball using the sand as a cushion since the contact point can be affected from different conditions in the bunker. Hitting out of wet sand his contact was much closer to the golf ball and would take a small amount of sand. On a plugged or buried ball he would shut down the face to take more sand, knowing the ball would run more on the green with no backspin. Moe could also hit a soft shot from a plugged lie by utilizing a steep angle to get into the sand with a longer swing that had spin. Normally it was spanking the sand as if a board was inches under the sand to keep the sole of the club on the same level.

My teacher was outstanding in the bunker and felt he could hole every shot or get it up and down. Moe wanted to keep the ball below the hole for an easy uphill putt. When faced with a long bunker shot from the fairway bunker he played the ball in the middle of his stance and used more upper body to minimize his leg action to hit the ball clean.

When Moe hit a short lofted shot from the fairway or going over a green side bunker, he would pull the end of the grip upward toward his left shoulder. This would elevate the golf ball higher and softer for delicate shots. His left wrist would stay upright and firm in the bowed position with the right hand along for the ride, passive and gradually working under the shot. Moe hit the golf ball at the height he visualized in his mind before he approached the shot. He never used his Sandy Andy off the fairway and only out of long rough around the green or for short bunker shots. Moe was also capable of hitting his pitching wedge better than most could hit a sand iron with adequate height or softness.

On chip shots from the apron Moe would select the club that would get the golf ball grounded early to clear the fringe with roll. His club selection would depend on the length of the chip shot. The more he wanted the ball to run, the less lofted club would be utilized. The seven, six or five irons were his normal choices that would provide adequate backspin particularly on larger contoured greens. Lastly, Moe had a pitching wedge cut shot in his bag for real softness.

Moe was a believer in keeping the club face square on short shot execution since the pitch shot is just a shorter version of the full golf swing. It was a common practice to go down the grip on his short shots or bunker shots for feel and control the same way he would hit the knock down shot when between clubs.

The knock down shot can be hit two ways. You can shorten the back swing or go down your grip where his preference was an inch and a half for full shots. Moe was a total control player on the course and through the green. Moe would say to me many times, "Never allow the golf ball to control you. I control the golf ball." It was drilled into me that good tempo on the short shots will continue into your long game and that will increase your percentages to score better.

Greg chipping with a six iron

Practicing my 60 yard wedge shot at Ashburn G.C. Halifax, Nova Scotia.

Spanking the sand with the Sandy wedge Moe gave me forty years ago.

Moe Norman Tournament Records

Murray (Moe) Irwin Norman (Born) July 10, 1929

Canadian Golf Hall of Fame 1995

Canada's Sport Hall of Fame 2006

(Died) September 4, 2004 (age 75)

International World Golf America's Cup Representing Canada

National Amateur

Canadian Amateur Champion 1955, 1956 Masters Invitation USA 1956

Canadian Open Runner- Up 1957 Masters Invitation USA 1957

Provincial Canadian Tour Stops

Ontario Open Champion 1958, 1963

Saskatchewan Open Champion 1963, 1968

Manitoba Open Champion 1965, 1966, 1967

Alberta Open Champion 1966, 1971, 1976

Canadian Professional Golfer's Association's National Tournaments

CPGA Miller Trophy 1964

CPGA Championship Runner- Up 1965 CPGA Championship Champion 1966 CPGA Championship Champion 1974

CPGA SENIORS Champion 1980,81,82,83,84,85,87

33 Course Records

17 Holes in One

Shot 59 Three Times

Four Double Eagles

Moe had his reasons for telling me the golf secrets he kept close to him. Those important jewels were Moe's treasures of greatness. When I saw Moe for the last time in Prince Edward Island he hoped I would write a book. Moe said to me, "Old buddy, I have told you everything I know and when the man upstairs takes me, you'll be the only one around that knows the golf swing I won all my tournaments with." The best pair of hands ever to hold a golf stick provided me with true friendship. It was an honor to FINISH TO THE SKY side by side with the greatest ball striker in the world for many years. God bless Moe for being Moe.

ABOUT THE AUTHOR —
Greg Lavern

In 1974 my close golf relationship with Moe Norman came to life through an introduction from Lawson Mitchell. From my confidential student relationship with Moe it could be said that I became known as the best kept secret in golf with world class knowledge. I had spent more time with Moe Norman learning the golf swing than anyone else in the world. During the seventies and eighties I was a member of the Canadian Professional Golfers Association with my final ten years of membership as a class "A" club professional.

Achievement of a Bachelor of Arts Degree and Diploma in Public Administration from the University of Prince Edward Island came years later. In 2002 I achieved a black belt in Chito Ryu karate and discovered the similarities between golf and the martial arts. While in my fifties I finalized my education with a Public Relations diploma from Eastern College Halifax, NS, Canada.

I still hit the golf ball the way Moe taught me with a total concentration on purity of technique. This book hopefully will inspire the golfing world with the proper procedure on how to really hit the golf ball solidly. It was my passion to honor Moe for all the private sessions he spent with me where together we would Finish To The Sky. This book should finalize his legacy. Moe Norman was the finest ball striker to play the game of golf.

Editor — Ian MacMillan

Having worked with Greg to take pictures and make videos of his swing I can testify to his remarkable ability with ball striking. From three drives he hit out to about 265 yards that I could have covered with a bath towel, to chipping with a tempo so smooth the video looked almost in slow motion.

When I introduced my wife to Greg at the small par 3 where he was at that time, he came out from behind the counter where he had been working most of the day and without so much as a warm up swing he hit three drives flush off of a practice putting surface without a tee. As Tim Lynch can verify, Greg is the real deal. He can not only talk about it, he can do it and show you how too.

If you are seriously considering improving your ball striking you don't have to look any further than this man who embodies the very swing Moe Norman was using when he was winning everything in sight. This book contains the three elements that, when understood, will transform your swing into something that will make you and your friends marvel, plus much, much more.

Made in the USA
Middletown, DE
26 September 2024

61467058R00087